Building Her House

Also by Nancy Wilson:

BOOKS

The Fruit of Her Hands
Respect and the Christian Woman

Our Mother Tongue
A Guide to English Grammar

Praise Her in the Gates
The Calling of Christian Motherhood

AUDIO SETS

Building Her House AudioBook

The Fruit of Her Hands AudioBook

Grandmas and Mothers-in-Law
On to the Next Thing

Keep It Simple
Scriptural Wisdom for Teenage Girls

Mothers and Daughters
Growing into Wise Women Together

The Pleasant Home
A Bible Study for Young Mothers

Praise Her in the Gates AudioBook

Visit www.canonpress.com for more details.

building *her* house

*commonsensical wisdom
for Christian women*

Nancy Wilson

canonpress
Moscow, Idaho

Published by Canon Press
P.O. Box 8729, Moscow, ID 83843
800-488-2034 | www.canonpress.com

Nancy Wilson, *Building Her House:*
Commonsensical Wisdom for Christian Women
Copyright © 2006 by Nancy Wilson

Cover credits: Photography by Mark LaMoreaux; photoshoppery by David
Dalbey; design by Laura Storm. Special thanks to La Bella Vita and Alison
Bradley. Interior design by Jared Miller and Laura Storm.

Library of Congress Cataloging-in-Publication Data

Wilson, Nancy
    Building her house : commonsensical wisdom for Christian women/
Nancy Wilson.
        p. cm.
    ISBN-13: 978-1-59128-039-2 (alk. paper)
    ISBN-10: 1-59128-039-7 (alk. paper)
    1. Mothers--Religious life. 2. Wives--Religious life. 3. Christian women--
Religious life. I. Title.
    BV4529.18.W555 2006
    248.8'43--dc22
                            2006027394

09 10 11 12 13 14 15   9 8 7 6 5 4 3 2

*Lovingly dedicated to my granddaughters
Jemima, Belphoebe, Hero, Lucia,
Ameera Margaret, Evangeline, and Daphne:*

*May you grow up to be mothers and grandmothers,
ever trusting in the God of your own mothers and
your own Nana.*

Contents

Part 5: Attitudes

Preface

$\diamond$

It was some time ago now—so long ago it makes me feel quite old—that my husband had one of my taped studies for women transcribed and put in a column titled "Femina." When he brought it home for my perusal, I was of course appalled by the writing—reading transcriptions is a very humbling experience for a speaker! But I got to work and cleaned it up so it could appear in the pages of *Credenda/Agenda*. So this is all really my husband's fault. He is the one who handed me that first column. He knew that if I saw it already on the page, even if it was in shabby condition, I would be far more inclined to think I could write a column for women. So I must thank him here for tricking me into writing.

Canon Press has kindly put together a collection of some of those essays, and here they are bound together. I have tried to arrange them under general headings, but I did not originally write them to organize in this way, so it is not a tight arrangement.

As we pray and labor for reformation in the church in America, we have to keep our eyes on the little things that are not as little as we think—things like feasting together around our tables, loving the little people in our families, and living sacrificially for one another. These seemingly "insignificant" duties are far more potent than we realize, for God sanctifies them and uses them to bless us, transform our communities, and bring glory to His name. It is my prayer that God might use these little essays to encourage faithfulness and joyfulness in the women who read them.

Part 1

Service

The Table

<><><><><><><><><><><><><><><><><><><><><><><><><><><><><><><><>

It's seen some wear and tear. In fact, I don't know what caused all the nicks, scratches, dents, and dings; some are real mysteries, like the puddle of small imprints that have textured one corner. The big gashes are more memorable than the dozens of small scrapes, pokes, and pits. The big ones can usually be attributed to some particular mishap or other, but all the random little blemishes blend into the swirl of meals and memories, shaping the story of our household, told around our table.

When we bought a pine table instead of a fine hardwood, I knew it would gain "character" quickly. But I also knew I wouldn't be tempted to fret over it. You expect a soft wood like pine to chronicle every activity, and besides, it was a fraction of the cost a beautiful mahogany table would be. Its broad yellow surface, cheerful and inviting, stretched out in bright contrast to the dark, shiny wood floors in our new house.

It seemed so huge at the time, so wide and hefty, and with the leaf in it, positively gigantic—a vast expanse filling our dining room with promise. The rounded legs, like tree trunks, bore its weight seemingly effortlessly. We were so impressed and pleased. Now this was a serious table. And because at the time all the living room had to offer in the way of seating was the floor and a lone rocking chair, the dining room table gained even more prominence and dignity. It truly became the center of all.

Isn't it a lovely oddity that we gather around our big piece of wood nearly every evening, about the same time each day, and eat a meal together? Sometimes it is an elegant meal. Sometimes it is very homely. But we are always there together, knife and fork in hand, doing our duty and rejoicing as we go. Oh, the hours of stories and jokes, questions and concerns (through courtships and pregnancies), prayers and discussions we have had around our aging table.

As the years have gone on, our table has shrunk. I don't know what happened. The living room filled up with furniture. Children married and began having babies. Though it seemed so roomy at first, now I'm wondering how we will all fit. Sometimes we squash five on each side and put two on each end. But just when it seems impossible to fit any more, we manage to slip six chairs on a side. We pull the high chair up to the corner. But soon one table won't be enough.

Disgraceful as it seems to the dignity of our table, we sometimes have to stoop to setting up a flimsy little card table off to the side. But who will sit there? No one wants to. Everyone wants to be at the big table. We've hauled a table up from the family room and arranged it in the living room, and we've put a table in the library. But this divides the festivities into two or three groups and causes longing looks from across the room.

One Easter we decided to make everyone happy, so we arranged one very long table downstairs. We borrowed folding tables and set them up the whole length of our family room. When the white tablecloths and candles and dishes and flowers and glasses were all arranged, it was quite spectacular. Everyone was pleased to be together, even if the conversation at one end was impossible to hear at the other. The picture of the One Table is deeply imbedded in us.

Since we managed to do it at Easter, we tried again for a Christmas family gathering we held on Boxing Day. Instead of putting the folding tables end to end, we grouped them so we had a long eight-foot wide table running the length of our family room. It was glorious. We filled the spacious middle section with fruit and candles and evergreen boughs. We hauled things up and down the stairs for days before and after. But it was worth all the labor to be around one big grand table.

But still, the pine table upstairs is my preference. It is humble now, not nearly as glorious as it once was. My grandchildren color pictures and roll out Play-Doh cookies on it. Clothes are folded on it. Groceries bags are piled on it. But it still holds candlelight and glistening wine glasses every Sabbath dinner when the whole family squashes around it and welcomes newcomers to the table. The babies babble (or even holler) and we pass them around; the toddlers sing and recite their memory verses for us. Just yesterday four generations sat down for lunch around our big pine table.

Modern middle-class homes seldom have separate, big dining rooms like the grand old houses of generations past. It's "wasted square footage" or too expensive. Besides, families are small and fragmented now. I remember a high-school friend who gave me a tour of her not-so-middle-class home. She pushed open some doors to reveal a beautiful room filled with antiques and a long shining table, chairs pushed in all around it. "This is the forbidden room," she told me. "We aren't allowed to go in here." And I could see why. But still, the principle of a glorious dining room appealed to me—so long as it wasn't a forbidden room, but rather a room for the whole family, where all could sit down together, if not every night, at least once a week, for a Sabbath feast.

When we celebrate the Lord's Supper each Lord's Day, I often think of the One Table that has been prepared for us, seeing it by faith. And our yellow pine table, with all its spots and blemishes, faintly pictures that perfect Table spread with God's Feast for all of us.

Sabbath Feasting

Sabbath dinner is a tradition at our house, but it hasn't always been that way. Shortly after our firstborn was married, we thought it would be nice to get together to kick off the Lord's Day, and there were just six of us, including our new son-in-law.

Though I would love to take credit for such a great idea as the Sabbath dinner, it was really Doug and Paula Jones who set the example for us. (Over the years they have quietly led by example in many wonderful things such as Sabbath dinners.) When we began to gather each Saturday night, we really had no idea what a great blessing this meal was going to become for us all. We had just moved into a new house, our daughter had just gotten married, and we had a large new table. It seemed the perfect time to make yet another change—beginning what was to us a very new practice of a weekly feast to celebrate the arrival of the Lord's Day.

One of the novel things about our newly established dinner was the presence of wine. I remember standing in the grocery store with no idea where to begin. What should I serve with what? One of those weeks I bumped into a friend with a whole lot more wine savvy than I had. Knowing we were new at this, he pointed me to an inexpensive sparkling wine that would not be too scary for us. I even had to invest in some wine glasses for the first time.

That was nearly ten years ago now, which isn't very long at all, and our Sabbath dinner has changed quite a bit. The most noticeable change is the number crowded around our new and bigger table. Not only has the adult population in the family grown to eight, but the little people outnumber us. With the increase of numbers has come the development of a liturgy, one I'm sure will change as the children grow older. When we visit friends' homes, we often come away with ideas to incorporate into our own dinner. Dave and Kim Hatcher sprinkle wrapped chocolates down the center of their table, and they play a story game between dinner and dessert that involves their kids. They also have a great way of teaching the children to wait for the hostess to take the first bite of dessert: If one of the children jumps in before the hostess, they pass that child's dessert around the table and everyone gets to take a bite! Steve and Jeannie Schlissel have a lovely way of welcoming everyone to their table that we have gratefully imitated. Doug and Paula Jones gave us the idea of having a liturgy to follow each week.

I have talked with many young mothers about how to get their Sabbath dinner going. One of the first things I try to do is dispel some myths about it. At our house, it is not Thanksgiving dinner every week with a turkey and all the trimmings. No way! Of course I try to make a meal that is a cut above the daily dinners. But it is not the same as an Easter or Christmas dinner where I pull out all the stops. The point is to start with what is feasible, not impossible. My children are grown, so I am not cooking with five little ones underfoot. Sabbath dinner ought to grow as your family does. Start small and work your way up. As your children get older and you have more help in the kitchen, you may be able to do more. The point is to celebrate the coming Lord's Day together in a festive manner around your table, week after week, all year long. If you start by using all your china, crystal, and fine linens, you may burn out after two weeks and give up. Ease in slowly.

Because my kids were college age when we started, I could pretty much do what I wanted. I had lots of help with the cleanup, and it was pretty simple. But as we've added high chairs and boosters, I have adjusted things accordingly. The college girls who live with us help in many ways. I have little wine glasses for the little people, lots of bibs, and always lots of rolls and honey butter. Dinners usually involve a big piece of meat coming out of the oven, but not always. It might be pasta or shish kebabs, and in the summer we eat outside as often as we can.

During the school year, I am cooking for twelve adults and ten children plus whatever company we have picked up, and it can reach (as it did last week) up to twenty-two adults. When that happens, the guests often help by bringing food or wine. The point in telling you all this is not to get you to do what we do, but rather to encourage you to just begin doing *something*. Your family will shape your Sabbath dinner into a unique weekly family feast. The point is to celebrate before the Lord around the table, knowing that He is preparing a table for all of us to sit down to where He will be seated at the head. We are simply practicing each week, preparing for the day when we will sit down with Him.

Your preparations for Sabbath dinner will be some of the most important work you do all week. Do it unto the Lord and ask Him to bless all your efforts by making your family look forward to it all week.

Mac and Cheese

◇◇

The Sabbath feast sets the tone for the rest of the week, making all those nightly gatherings around the table even sweeter. Although the Sabbath feast usually involves a large piece of meat and various side dishes, other more humble dinners are just as much a part of the family's history and heritage. Macaroni and cheese enjoys that status at our house, so I feel it is my duty to speak of the glories of Velveeta when the family is yearning for some real down-home comfort food. It is a staple food for young families, along with peanut-butter-and-jelly sandwiches. And I'm not talking about the kind of mac and cheese you buy in a box for a quarter. No, no, no. That might be fine for hungry college students, and my grandkids adore it for lunch. I am talking about the real deal: home-cooked mac and cheese made with Velveeta.

My daughter found a recipe for "Uptown Getdown Macaroni and Cheese" that calls for eight different kinds of real cheeses and costs about fifteen dollars to make. It is good enough to serve to company with a nice mellow red wine. That's great for some occasions, but I am speaking here of the golden, gooey stuff that comes out of the oven covered with steaming brown bubbles. Make a bowl of this and your five-year-old (or twenty-five-year-old!) will think you are an angel.

This kind of macaroni and cheese is good left over, even straight out of the fridge, still in the big Dutch oven or huge Pyrex bowl. Tradition at my house involves the big, blue, porcelain-covered, cast-iron Dutch oven my parents bought in Holland. I grew up watching delectable things come out of that big Dutch oven. Now it resides in my cupboard, and it is the vessel of choice for macaroni and cheese. It will hold a double batch easily.

I know that Velveeta can be used for things like cheese soup, and it does melt nicely for a grilled cheese sandwich, but I still prefer other cheeses for these uses. When it comes to macaroni and cheese, however, Velveeta is the good stuff.

Depending on how or where you grew up, macaroni is served with ketchup. I didn't grow up with macaroni and cheese regularly on the menu. Mom was a great cook, and I mostly remember a lot of pot roasts and mashed potatoes. But I also remember that Dad could whip up a mess of macaroni and cheese that could compete with the best. He's the one who taught me to put ketchup on my macaroni and cheese, and so I grew up assuming everyone else did. I really don't know if he used Velveeta, or if it had even been invented yet in the fifties and sixties.

My husband grew up with a different macaroni and cheese tradition. In fact, after we were married I got his mom's recipe so I could perform the mac and cheese ritual appropriately. I had not thought about macaroni and cheese for years, and I had certainly never made it from scratch.

The crisp brown edge of the mac and cheese stuck on the edge of the pan was much prized in his house. They did not douse it with ketchup and were a bit shocked at my addition. I'm afraid our children (and grandchildren) have taken after my side of the family. You simply don't serve mac and cheese unless you have ketchup on hand. It does spoil the color somewhat, but it still looks good on the plate next to some green peas. And it's helpful for teaching the children what happens when you add red to yellow—you get orange.

Years ago we had unexpected company stop by. I soon realized this family of good size wasn't really stopping by, but planned on staying for the next meal. I also realized I didn't have the volume of ingredients on hand to offer anything very impressive for dinner. Then it came to me: macaroni and cheese. I made a blue vat of it. Everyone was happy, and the kids especially loved it. We passed the ketchup.

The glory of macaroni and cheese is its comfort level. It is cheap and even nutritious, doesn't take long to make, and is quite filling. Babies can eat it. Old people can eat it. It has simple ingredients: milk, butter, flour, salt and pepper, cheese, and the noodles. Even the most inexperienced cook can produce a big casserole dish of it. If you want to be rather gourmet about it, you can add a little Worcestershire or mustard powder to the cheese sauce. I once heard of someone adding raisins, but it was not well-received.

Today macaroni and cheese has made a comeback. You can find dozens of recipes online, and many new cookbooks even include a recipe. The ultimate comfort food, these newer recipes are often far more sophisticated than my old Velveeta recipe. Some call for Swiss cheese or even mozzarella. Some put bread crumbs on the top. Ina Garten includes a recipe in her *Family Style* cookbook (a *New York Times* bestseller) that uses Gruyère and extra-sharp Cheddar. (The only thing that worries me about her recipe is the half teaspoon of nutmeg.) She adds sliced tomatoes and bread crumbs on the top to make it snazzier, but even my old *Better Homes and Gardens Cookbook* from the seventies suggests the sliced, salted tomatoes on the top.

Though I've never served macaroni and cheese for a Sabbath dinner yet, I am not against it in principle. The point of Sabbath dinner is to celebrate the Lord's Day together with family and friends, and all with a spirit of rejoicing and thanksgiving. Though a big piece of roasted meat is always welcome at the table, I doubt any of my family would be disappointed if I brought out the big blue Dutch oven full of steaming macaroni and cheese. The Lord is Lord of all.

Perfectly Domestic

In the world of platonic domesticity, everything runs like clockwork. The children all rise up at the same time each morning, arrive at the breakfast table promptly and dressed appropriately, and then begin to check off the chores one by one on the list posted on the fridge door. Soon they all assemble, homework in hand, ready to leave for school, or they sit down at their desks at home, all attention and cheerfulness, ready to begin their daily studies. Throw in morning worship somewhere in there, and add tidying up their bedrooms, and we have the platonic form of the perfectly-run, "godly" home. The only problem is that so many homes like this can be perfect hell-holes.

Now I'm not against being organized. But we have to model our homes after the style of our Creator, not after the style of a robot or a computer. How does God organize His world? Into precise days, minutes, hours, and seconds. But also into seasons and lifetimes, sunrise, sunset, spring and fall, winter and harvest, full moons, and summer thunderstorms. My husband is fond of saying that God is perfect, but He is not a perfectionist. Perfectionism is man's invention. And some well-meaning saints can fall into the temptation of trying to achieve so-called perfection by means of their well-ordered schedules which they impose on everyone around them.

The sun does not get up at the same time every day. But he does get up. The sun doesn't even set at the same time every day, but we always have a sunset. Sometimes spring is early, sometimes late. Snow arrives in October one year and stays until March, but then never shows up at all, not even for Christmas, the very next year. God's world is generally predictable, but not *exactly* predictable. If the weather teaches us anything, it is that God is in charge and He does as He pleases.

Now how does this translate into overseeing our domestic responsibilities? Am I saying we should be unpredictable, never serving dinner up at the same time two days in a row? Of course not. But at the same time, we should not get stressed out about many of the details. When we say dinner is at six, it should come out of the oven sometime around six, give or take a few minutes, and we should not worry over such things. Am I saying it doesn't matter if your husband shows up to work on time or not? Of course it matters. But if he is extremely punctual to the second, he is not spiritually superior to the man who is occasionally a couple minutes late. Our flesh wants to take pride in the dumbest things.

This has particular application in raising children. Life should be generally predictable for them. This gives them security and makes them feel loved and cared for. But the schedule should never become more important than they are. I seem to remember the Lord saying something like this: "The schedule was made for man, not man for the schedule." If keeping to the schedule is an ongoing temptation and source of friction in the home, then the schedule is a snare and a trap. If parents think they are godly if they "run a tight ship," but the children are like the Von Trapp family before Maria arrived, then all is not well. Real godliness can discern the difference between external conformity to the rules and a heart overflowing with delight in obedience. Wisdom knows when the schedule needs to be ignored, stretched, or thrown out all together.

The spiritual snare in these kinds of situations has to do with self-approval. If we have a regimented home life with every hour planned, we can find satisfaction with ourselves when we have stuck to our schedule, and we view our children as godly when they check off their daily list of duties. But then we are tempted to overlook our bad heart attitudes that come out when we snap at the kids, jerk them by the shoulder, glower at them when they don't do what they are told, scold and correct them for less than instant obedience, while all along we are disobeying the biggies right before their eyes. When we go beyond snapping and scolding and even yell at the kids over something like leaving their shoes in the wrong place, something is seriously out of order, and it's not the shoes. This scenario can be the result of a self-imposed pressure to keep everything in its place, including the children.

But the errors are never just on one side. Some families could use a good dose of scheduling to calm some of the chaos in their homes and provide a little order and stability. And even those families who just career from one thing to the next can sin by feeling superior to the families who in their opinion are much too tidy. The balance comes when we take ownership of our very own particular sins and weaknesses by confessing them to God. Only then we can learn from one another, discipline our own troubles, and not compare ourselves to our neighbor, either to gloat or to feel inferior.

In the average home there is much work to be done, and God does not approve of laziness. But beware thinking that your schedule (whether it is a homeschooling schedule or feeding-the-baby schedule) is inspired by the Holy Spirit. Life in our homes should be characterized by joy and thanksgiving so that children are taught and nourished in a way that takes their souls into account.

Loving Labor

<><><><><><><><><><><><><><><><><><><><><><><><><><><><><><><><><><><><><><><>

In the last chapter of Romans, Paul mentions all the people he wants to greet, and he commends some of those by name who have been of particular help to him. Early in this list, Paul mentions Mary: "Greet Mary, who bestowed much labour on us" (Rom. 16:6).

This woman apparently ministered to Paul and his coworkers in a wonderful way. We can only imagine the sort of needs Paul and his entourage had as they traveled. The obvious of course would be food and a place to sleep. But Paul would also probably attract crowds of people who would want to listen to him teach. So Mary's hospitality may have extended beyond just Paul and those traveling with him. Whatever the case, it is obvious that Paul took special note of Mary's hospitality, for it was a blessing to him.

Notice that Mary *bestowed* her labor. What a lovely word. It suggests the image of a gift. This means her hospitality was not given grudgingly or sparingly. It is as though all her labor was wrapped up, tied with a ribbon, and given with the anticipation of delighting and pleasing. Hospitality that is *bestowed* is the sort the Scripture exhorts us to practice: "Use hospitality one to another without grudging" (1 Pet. 4:9). Grudging hospitality is not a joy to receive.

Mary bestowed much labor, not a little labor. And it *was* labor—real labor. Anyone who doesn't think hospitality is work has much to learn about giving. Mary's work probably included anticipating and preparing, organizing and directing, as well as spending hours in the kitchen and cleaning up. Though hospitality is a joy, it is labor-intensive. Paul was wise enough to know that Mary was working hard to provide for his needs. Hospitality is a precious gift, for it is the sacrifice of someone's time and energy.

So what can we learn from Mary's example? First we must learn to bestow our gifts and services on our fellow saints. When God in His kindness establishes a loving, healthy Christian community, much hard work of serving one another is required among the saints. This may include putting people up, feeding them, loaning them cars, driving them to the airport, visiting them when they are sick, taking them meals, babysitting their children, buying them shower gifts, or shoveling their walks. Not only is a thriving church community dependent upon the labors of the saints to maintain it, but its very existence speaks of years of labor and self-sacrifice that have gone into merely establishing it. Communities do not just spring up out of thin air; they are always the result of hard work over many years. Great blessings always require careful stewardship, and this necessarily mandates much labor—a good deal of which may be completed behind the scenes.

Scripture teaches that it is more blessed to give than receive. If you have ever been on the receiving end, as Paul was, you know how much of a blessing the labors of others can be. And if you have ever been very needy, as Paul was, you know how difficult it is to be left to fend for yourself. And yet, as blessed as it is to receive when we are needy, it is more blessed to be the giver. A healthy Christian community is characterized by people who labor for one another, looking after the needs of others (Phil. 2:4).

Though men and women alike have many opportunities to serve others, women are uniquely suited for bestowing labor on the saints. We can strive to provide for their needs in thoughtful ways, whatever it is they need, in order to make their load easier to bear. Though we may not be privileged to have an apostle in our home, we are privileged to serve all kinds of people God puts in our path. Hebrews 13:2 tells us, "Be not forgetful to entertain strangers: for thereby some have entertained angels unawares." Third John 5–8 also mentions entertaining brothers and strangers and helping them on their way.

But serving has its temptations, like everything else in this fallen world. We can labor as an end in itself instead of as a means to glorifying God. This is when we become too focused on the event and not on the people. We can become tired, distracted, and discouraged with "much serving" like Martha. We forget that we are "bestowing." This can happen when we put together a big Christmas or Thanksgiving feast for many people, only to realize we have to feed them all again in the morning.

We may be eager to "bestow" labor upon some people who are very appreciative and want to reciprocate, but what about those who won't provide much of a return? Some saints (or family members) don't seem to notice our "great labor" for them, but Jesus says to invite those who cannot repay us (Lk. 14:12).

Mothers bestow great labor on their families day in and day out. They do many things that no one seems to notice. Who sees the messes cleaned up, the noses wiped, the pots washed, and all the other labor of managing the home? This is where it is necessary to remember Christ's words on the subject: "Inasmuch as ye have done it unto one of the least of these my brethren, ye have done it unto me" (Mt. 25:40).

Many times what is needed is a perspective adjustment. As women look at all their labor, they need to see what it really is that they are bestowing. Whether the recipients of all the great labor are family members, fellow church-members, traveling saints, or strangers, it should be seen as a privilege to bestow our labor upon them. It is a good work that not only blesses the giver and the receiver, but honors God and brings Him glory.

Part 2
Family Relationships

Courtship Blues

◇◇

So it isn't a fairy-tale world after all. You read the courtship books and thought it sounded so easy. Maybe it was at first, but then the crash came. The whole thing fell through, blew up, unraveled, and came to a screeching halt. And whether you are the mother or the daughter, you still feel devastated and embarrassed that what seemed to be a good idea at the time obviously wasn't. There goes your idea of the perfect couple and the perfect courtship. But before you give up on the whole idea, consider a few things first.

Courtship is supposed to be the time to find out if you are right for this person. It is not the wedding-planning segment of the relationship. That is called the *engagement*. Courtship is a time for two people to get acquainted in a non-threatening manner, with parental oversight. It is a time for getting to know each other. It is a time for finding out. If, after a few weeks of "finding out," you find you are not interested, then it is not a disgrace. It is not a sign of failure. It is not even a huge deal. Unless, of course, you have made it a huge deal by making courtship more than it ought to have been.

One of the first ways to wreck a courtship is to start acting like it is an engagement. Parents can do this by running ahead when they should be exercising wisdom and caution by checking to see how their daughter is doing and by getting to know the young man who is doing the courting. Well-meaning friends do the same thing when they start congratulating the couple and asking about the honeymoon. All of this exerts undue and unkind pressure on the couple. It changes the tone of the relationship from low-key to high-pressure. It makes the two people involved feel like they must resolve all their issues immediately. Often this is not possible, so one or the other asks to please be excused. So ends the courtship.

Another "creative" way to trash a courtship is for the couple to get too physically involved too fast (as in, at all). Some dads allow no physical contact; some dads allow some. Some dads aren't watching. When it finally comes to light that there has been way too much going on, someone usually blows the whistle and calls the whole thing off. And because of the physical intimacy, there is much emotional damage. This is more often the case when the courtship has been allowed to drag on far too long. This sometimes comes from parents wanting their sixteen-year-old to be in a courtship, even though they will not consider marriage for several years. Such an arrangement increases all the hazards.

Some parents think courtship is simply a form of entertainment for their offspring, and so they allow or encourage their daughters to be courted by several men over several years. For various reasons, none of these courtships end in marriage, but it sounds great on the resume to say you have courtship "experience." Why not just go back to recreational dating? At least in the dating system no one expects you to be serious about the relationship, and no one is surprised at the breakup.

Some courtships fail because of too many idealistic assumptions from the outset. The daughter visualizes her own personal dream relationship, and when this solid Christian man doesn't sweep her off her feet or swing her up onto his horse as he rides by, she calls it off. She wants more fireworks, or she wishes he were more like some man in her imagination. This unfortunate scenario can be caused by indulging in too much cheap fiction or by simply being too immature to handle a serious relationship.

As long as I am venting about this, I may as well include the overeager parents who thrust their daughter into a courtship she

is not ready for. She may be a submissive daughter who is striving
to please her parents, but as the relationship continues, she may
buckle under the pressure. Parents should not cause such misery.
They are supposed to be the means God uses to protect their
daughters, not the means of inflicting suffering. A daughter who
is marrying for no other reason than to please her parents is in
grave danger indeed. Who wants a martyr for a wife?

And of course, sometimes even when the courtship is con-
ducted in an honorable fashion from start to finish, it still doesn't
end with a wedding. If courtship really is a time for "finding out,"
then sometimes the couple will find out they just don't click or
jive. So a courtship can end with good feelings all around, even
if there is a bit of disappointment. This is not a big disgrace. It's
just a bump in the road and can be easily overcome. If you haven't
made it a huge deal, it won't be a huge deal.

In spite of all these sad and miserable endings, courtship does
have a lot going for it. Consider, for instance, that when all cyl-
inders are running, Dad keeps daughter from having to do the
dirty work. He says "no" for her whenever it is appropriate. She
doesn't have to fend the guys off; Dad does it. If the courtship
ends, Dad can do the breaking up for his daughter. She doesn't
have to explain or defend. Dad does. This is a glorious aspect of
courtship that can protect not only the daughter, but also the fine
fellow who has been behaving like a gentleman. It's far easier for
a young man to deal with another male, even if that other male
is telling him (however nicely) to get lost. And it's funny how
dads understand the issues and can communicate them squarely.
Of course, I have to admit here that there are exceptions; there
are dads who cannot be trusted. But let's hope we are not dealing
with that sort here.

Courtship should be an exciting time for all involved, but it
should also be a time for honesty and restraint. Don't give yourself
unnecessary headaches by treating it as something more, or less,
than what it is.

Mother-in-Law

◇◇

As we look forward to our children being married, we have to realize it means a change in the job description for us moms. Of course this has been happening all along: What a mother does for her infant is vastly different from what she does for her toddler or teenager. Becoming a mother-in-law is just another wonderful promotion. But like everything else, it is accompanied with unique temptations.

What is the stereotypical mother-in-law noted for? We all know this part of our cultural catechism very well. She is domineering, critical, opinionated, and a pain to be around. So the obvious biblical conclusion to draw from this is "Don't be like that." Sounds easy, doesn't it? Well, actually it is, if we really think about it. We all have access to God's Word, we have the Holy Spirit to enable us to be obedient and godly, and we have a Savior who forgives us when we ask. It is also a great blessing if you have children and children-in-law who are also quick to forgive, because you are going to need it.

Mothers are used to giving "input" to their children from the time they are born. Of course we are to taper off as they become young adults, but the temptation is going to be to continue after they are married. But it is imperative that parents not be critical of either their grown children or in-laws. Lay off. Let love cover it! Of course your in-law children did not grow up in your home, so they will do things differently. Learn to enjoy these differences. If you see something that is clearly ungodly, pray about it. Ask God to deal with it, but only after you have asked Him to deal with you first. Maybe you are not seeing the whole picture. Maybe it isn't as bad as you think. Maybe you are being a fuss-budget. Do not offer your two cents unless you are asked. Though you felt free to teach and instruct your children when they were growing up, it is now time to be done. You had your chance—now be quiet.

Replace your criticism with gratitude. Thank your in-law children for all the wonderful things they do. Praise them! Tell your son what a sweet wife he has; tell your daughter how thankful you are for that husband of hers. No matter what faults you may see, there are far more virtues for you to rejoice in than faults. But if you have a critical spirit, you are blinded to many of the graces that may be obvious to everyone else. Repent of your critical spirit and ask God to replace it with thanksgiving and appreciation. Start using your tongue to build up, encourage, and praise. And remember that a critical attitude can be expressed by a look or a tone of voice, even if you are not saying specifically negative words.

Don't take personally your kids' and in-laws' decisions about what they do in their family. This is so important, so let me explain. Perhaps you homeschooled your children at great personal sacrifice. Now that they are grown, married, and have their own children, maybe they are thinking about using the local Christian school to educate their kids. Don't blow up. Don't freak out. Don't be negative. Think of how you can help contribute toward their tuition, and make sure you go to every event your grandchildren are involved in, whether it is the Christmas program, Grandparents Day, or all those basketball games.

Likewise, if you sacrificed to start a Christian school for your own kids, but now they want to homeschool their own children, don't take it personally. It doesn't mean they don't appreciate all you did for them. Think of ways to help pay for the books and supplies. Help out on the field trips. Be a hands-on grandma who is a cheerleader for your children no matter what. Nothing alienates your children from you quicker than being critical of the choices they make regarding their own children, whether it is

birthing at home or at a hospital, educational choices, childrearing decisions, alternative medical decisions, and so forth. Your
kids need your support, not your icy stare.

Many young married couples are worrying years in advance
about how their parents are going to take it when they tell them
what they have decided to do about X, Y, or Z. This only com-
plicates their decision making. So set them free by taking the
initiative. Say something like, "Look, we educated you in the
classical Christian school, but you may decide to homeschool. We
want you to know that we will support you one-hundred percent
whatever you decide to do. Don't ever worry that we'll be upset
if you don't do it the same way we did. You are the parents, and
you can count on us to cheer you on all the way."

Imagine the tremendous sigh of relief on the part of your children. They will delight in being around you and love telling you
what they are planning and doing with their kids, because they
will know your love is unconditional and has no strings attached
to any particular method. This is simply the golden rule. Many
of you remember what it was like to feel your own parents' dis-
approval regarding these issues. Don't do to your kids what you
wished your parents hadn't done to you.

Don't impose expectations on your married children when it
comes to holidays, either. Set them free to spend time together as
a family, to go to the other set of in-laws for Christmas, or to come
to your house. Tell them you are flexible. Don't make them promise to be at your house. Share, don't demand. Don't put a guilt trip
on them about how disappointed Aunt Suzie will be. Concentrate
on making them feel welcome any time. And don't feel competi-
tive with the other set of in-laws in trying to out-give.

Enjoy the fact that God has established a new household for
your children and respect and honor them in it. God—and your
children—will bless you for it.

Daughter-in-Law

Daughters-in-law don't have nearly as much bad press that mothers-in-law have, and I'm not sure that is entirely just. They have it in their power to make the lives of their mothers-in-law full of joy or trouble, and like all women in every station, they can turn to God's Word for clear wisdom and direction.

The Bible is emphatic that children are to honor their parents. I do not think it is a stretch to apply this same command to in-laws. A daughter should honor her parents, and a married daughter should honor her husband's parents in the same way. She should do this unto the Lord, but not because she automatically feels the same way toward her mother-in-law that she does toward her own mother. No one expects a married woman to suddenly become as attached to her husband's mother as she is to her own. But she should still strive to show a great respect for and bestow a special kind of honor on her mother-in-law. This means that a married woman will be courteous, kind, and thoughtful toward her mother-in-law in the same way she would be to her own mother. In fact, because she has years of an established relationship with her own mother, she may need to go above and beyond to make her mother-in-law feel loved and appreciated. In doing so, however, she must take care not to neglect her own mother.

Courtesy implies graciousness and politeness. And what is graciousness but extending God's grace into our manners, so we are not stiffly polite but rather genuinely warm and friendly? Courtesy involves treating others as you would wish to be treated, and it includes the way you talk to and about your mother-in-law (even to your husband). Ask your husband to help you get to know her better. He can interpret her if you are confused. He can guide you in establishing a solid relationship with her.

Kindness encompasses everything from regular phone calls and cards to caring for her when she is ill or helping her pick up the groceries. It is sympathetic and generous, looking for ways to be charitable and tender-hearted. It is quick to forgive and unwilling to bear a grudge. Kindness doesn't take offense if your mother-in-law offers advice—even without your asking!—but receives it with humility instead of defensiveness.

And thoughtfulness includes your mother-in-law in the wonderful blessings of your married life, namely your children. Sometimes it is a juggle to balance time with both sets of grandparents. But strive to see that your children have the benefit of time with both sets of grandparents. Adapt to your in-laws' style. Maybe they would love to babysit for you. If so, take them up on it. But if they don't, then don't impose on them.

I occasionally remind young married women that they have taken a new name and their children will bear this name. Though they should of course continue to nurture and enjoy the relationship they have with their own parents, it is important that they really leave and cleave. Your mother-in-law did the same thing that you have done: She left her father and her mother, and she married a man with this same last name. She has been grafted into this family tree the same way you have been. You really have a lot in common. Of course Ruth exemplifies this beautifully for us: "Thy people shall be my people, and thy God, my God" (Ruth 1:16b). Few women today are in the same straits as Ruth, but the principle of her stalwart identification with her mother-in-law is a good subject for our reflection.

You can identify with your husband's family in many ways. Find out your husband's family history. Make an effort to visit his extended family. Gather up the old family recipes from the great-grandmothers and find out about the family traditions. Make your mother-in-law know that you are honored to bear the same last name. Not only will your husband be pleased to see you reverencing his family and his name, but your children will grow up knowing the family stories and being proud of their heritage.

Don't compare your mother-in-law to your mother. As my own mother-in-law says, "Comparisons are odious." You want to be thankful to God for the woman she is, not discontented or wishing she were different or more like your own mother. The fact that she is the mother of your husband should in itself make you grateful. Thank her for all she did in raising him to be the kind of man you wanted to marry. Learn from her. I'm sure there is plenty she has to offer that would be of benefit to you. Ask her to tell you about her son, and *listen*. Listening does not require that you agree with everything; instead, it is an active way of honoring her.

Now some of this might seem too much like a fairy tale. I know there can be serious family problems. If your mother-in-law is a real pain in the neck, and you are not imagining things, you are still called to honor her. You can return good for evil, you can let love cover a multitude of sins, and you can pray for much grace to be kind to her for the Lord's sake. If she is not trustworthy, then I am certainly not suggesting you let her babysit the kids anyway. But even with the most difficult situations, you can strive to be a faithful daughter-in-law, looking for opportunities to treat her with kindness for the Lord's sake and for your husband's sake. God always blesses our obedience to Him when it is rendered in faith.

We have all seen the fruit of persevering love in tough situations. God has given you one particular mother-in-law to honor. She may be a delight or she may be a challenge. Either way, you are called to be a good steward of the opportunity you have to be a source of blessing to your mother-in-law. And by being a blessing to her, you will be a blessing to future generations.

Part 3
Marriage

Young Wives

After all the hubbub of the engagement, the wedding planning, the actual event, the honeymoon, and the settling in, a young wife may experience a period of real adjustment. She has a new name and a new job assignment. The transition from daughter to wife is understandably a big one—her whole identity has changed. Soon the excitement of unpacking the wedding gifts and moving into a new place gives way to the everyday schedule and seemingly mundane duties of keeping the home. It's one thing to have strong views about the glorious calling of vocational domesticity; it is another thing altogether to live it out, day after day.

Particularly if the young wife is not working outside the home, she may find that she can accomplish her duties in short order, leaving her with more free time than she knows what to do with. (Of course some of you will rightly say here that there is always more that can be done. Even though that may be the case, for a young woman who has not yet hit her stride, she may not see it yet.) And if the Lord does not send her children right away, she may wonder what God wants her doing with her time. And now is a perfect opportunity for all the lies about lack of fulfillment for women who stay home to rear their ugly heads. "So what do you do now that you are married?" people ask. And when the answer is not to their satisfaction, there is the look of pity and wonder. Now the doubts appear: "What am I doing anyway?" Though each situation will vary considerably, here are a few considerations and thoughts to keep the young wife's perspective focused.

First of all, don't be surprised if it takes a while for you to get your feet under you. All big changes require a little time to get comfortable. Flexibility is a wonderful attribute to pray for. Meanwhile, don't be hard on yourself or impatient. It's not a sin to be a little thrown by a new schedule, a new town, a new house, or even a new husband. He may not be so good at it yet either. You're learning together. Take it easy.

Next, don't give way to discontent. Give yourself a good job description. Don't allow little doubts and ugly attitudes to creep in, saying things like, "I thought marriage would be different," or "It's not the way I thought it would be." Don't turn into a complainer. This includes not camouflaging your complaining to look like "sharing" with the girls. Don't spread the news of your discontent around town. It's amazing how fast the word gets out. This kind of complaining is simply disrespecting your husband. Complaining only makes things worse, and it has the additional benefit of making you no fun to be around. This is the proverbial drippy-faucet woman who makes life miserable for her husband and everyone else around her. No wonder he may be tempted to think, "What happened to the woman I married?" And since he is inexperienced and does not yet know how to deal with an unhappy wife, he may start to find excuses to work late. So begins the big mess.

Neither should you turn into a couch potato. If you really don't have enough to do, find a fruitful use for your time. Don't start filling up idle hours with useless activities like too much internet time, idiotic novels, overeating, soap operas, or gossiping on the phone. These are not neutral activities, but destructive and spiritually unhealthy. Women with too much time on their hands can become overspenders as well as overeaters. Though shopping is one of a wife's duties, she can squander money by spending it carelessly and frivolously.

If a woman is flourishing in her home and glorifying God while rejoicing in her domestic duties, and doing them well, but still finding extra hours in her day, she is in a position to look for more to do. She has something to export. This might be volunteer work for the community or church, it may be part-time employment, or it might be learning new skills at home. The possibilities are endless when we really think about it. A new wife may be able to ease gradually into assuming more responsibilities outside the home as she becomes more and more proficient at the job God has given her, but it is unwise to do this too quickly.

Sometimes a woman can kid herself into thinking she has extra time, when in fact she is actually just barely getting by with the minimum in her basic domestic duties. For example, if she simply rotates three dinners over and over because that's all she knows how to make, her problem is not that she has too much time on her hands. She needs help and input and encouragement, not outside activities to give her more to do. She has to determine to become skilled at the tasks God has assigned her.

In this case, she ought to be looking for ways to spend time with some of the older women she knows who can teach her how to cook. Not only will this give her more to do, but it is a productive use of her time and will be a mutual blessing both to her and to the women who teach her to cook, or can, or sew, or garden, or whatever it is. This will in turn build the young woman's confidence and expertise, making her not only more capable, but also more content with her job.

Submission

◇◇

The world regards the idea of wives submitting to their husbands as archaic, repressive, and obnoxious. When unbelievers attend a Christian wedding, they are sometimes appalled at references to that "dirty word" *submit*, or even worse, *obey*. They think the world has better ideas about marriage. This is funny, really—the world has trashed marriage, sex, and the family in a spectacular way.

We know that God is the Creator of marriage, not man. He has made it clear in His Word what He expects of both wives and husbands. Our duties are laid out for us, and He always blesses obedience. Faithful Christian marriages are bright lights that defy the lies of a dark, dark world.

But sad to say, many Christian marriages are not the bright lights they should be. Both husbands and wives refuse to obey the Word: Husbands fail to take responsibility, and wives behave in disrespectful ways. In spite of the fact that the church has emphasized teaching on marriage and the family, much still needs to be done. And when Christians are disobedient, the Word of God is blasphemed. Titus 2:3–5 makes this very clear. When Christian women are taught to be "discreet, chaste, keepers at home, good, [and] obedient to their own husbands," God is glorified. And Paul says here the result is "that the word of God be not blasphemed." Not only is the world guilty of this blasphemy, but Christian wives are as well, for ungodly behavior is by nature blasphemous. So wives become guilty of disrespecting God and His Word.

Often women who know better are failing to be respectful, dutiful, submissive, and obedient wives. They make excuses for their behavior, saying things like, "Well, I know it wasn't very respectful, but he was wrong." But if the older Christian women don't know how to obey their husbands, how can they teach the younger women? In this way the church is sick and passing the infection on to the next generation. Finally, sometimes wives think they understand respect, but they fail at the obedience part. "What do you mean I have to obey him? I thought that was just for the children."

But returning to the passage in Titus, older women are to teach younger women to be "obedient to their own husbands." Obedience is something wives should be practicing so they can teach it to others. This means obedience in everything, not just in the big things and not just in the little things. Good Christian wives need to learn to obey.

It is amazing how much we gloss over this and how much we excuse and overlook. The commands of submission and obedience are only difficult when we disagree with our husbands. If we agree with them and do what they say, it can hardly be called *submission*. Submission comes into play when we differ with them over an issue, but we defer to them and willingly give way.

But what about when the husband is in sin? This is a very important issue. What if the husband has adopted a wrong attitude and is heading in the wrong direction? Is a wife obligated to go along? It all depends. I have often been saddened that we don't see more Abigails in the church today. She was not afraid to call her husband a fool and make arrangements behind his back without his permission. God blessed her abundantly for intervening in this way. She did not stay home and wait for David to attack her household while calling herself a submissive wife. She recognized that her husband was acting the part of a fool, and she exercised wisdom and prudence by going to King David herself.

If a man is acting foolishly, a woman is foolish to go along quietly. Of course this requires great wisdom. I am not advocating giving wives license to disobey in a willy-nilly fashion; that is what I am objecting to in the paragraphs above. But there are times when a godly wife should beseech her husband not to act in a foolish manner. It may involve doctrine. Perhaps she is alarmed that he is being attracted to heretical ideas, whether it is "openness theology" or Roman Catholicism. She should speak to him respectfully about this and let him know she cannot follow him there. If she belongs to a godly church, her elders would support her in this.

Perhaps he is plotting to create some kind of stink in the church. Abigail would not stand for it. A good Christian wife should go to the elders and ask them how she can be a good church member and a good wife at the same time. She should not simply stand by, hoping that her husband will do the right thing. Nor should she just accept anything her husband does as though he is infallible. If a husband is bad-mouthing his elders, his pastor, or his friends, a godly woman should refuse to go along. She should speak to him privately first, but if he is not receptive, she should go to her pastor or elders and seek their advice. This same pattern should be followed if a husband is violent, if he has a temper, if he is cheating on his income taxes, if he is not providing for the household, or if he is being sexually unfaithful in any way—and this is not an exhaustive list.

A wife is to be a helper to her husband, not a blind follower, and this sometimes involves going past him to get help. God blessed Abigail when she did this. In her case it was abundantly clear what was necessary. In other cases it might require pastoral input and oversight. But obedience and submission to a mere man is never absolute. God governs all of us. We demonstrate that we serve Him above all others when we realize that our submission and obedience to our husbands is always to be lived out within the boundaries God has wisely set for us.

Big Stinking Tangles

Sometimes marriage difficulties are so tangled that it takes a lot of patience and faith to even begin the process of sorting them out and loosening all the knots that have accumulated. With a ball of string that is full of snarls, it is tempting to just go get the scissors, cut out the mess, and start over. In the case of a Christian marriage covenant, however, that is not necessarily the only way out. (I am not speaking here of the exceptions allowed by Scripture for adultery.)

The flesh wants to ditch, bale, skip out, start over, get even, get a life, think about me, give up, and move on. But once disobedience gets on a roll, it only leads downhill to more and more sin, unhappiness, and misery, until it finally crashes into a little heap somewhere. I've seen this more than once in real life. In fact, sometimes things are so messed up that a Christian wife deliberately sins in a flamboyant manner, just so the church or her husband will be forced to excommunication or divorce or both.

Of course, biblical repentance is what is needed, but a heart that is overtaken in sin rarely wants to admit its own guilt. It is far easier to focus on the sins of the other person, whether real or imagined, and there is usually plenty to complain about. A hard heart is a frightening thing to behold. It justifies disobedience by assigning all the blame to others. It grows more and more vindictive, unreasonable, and self-centered, if that is possible. A heart hardened by sin begins to embrace behavior that it once knew to be wicked. Compromise follows compromise, until it seems there

is no way to bring the person back. Discussion doesn't work. A
hard heart makes for a very muddled brain that does not respond
to reason or pleading.

Only the resurrecting grace and power of God can bring about
the kind of all-encompassing, all-out repentance that is urgently
needed in such cases. A fleshly kind of "I'm sorry" won't accomplish anything. This kind of soul-destroying cancer requires a
thorough removal that only God's grace can bring about.

So, what can be done? First consider a few very simple pre-
ventative measures. Confess your sins on a regular, daily basis.
Do not allow bitterness and resentment to get a foothold in your
heart and mind. Certainly, in some marriages there will be many
provocations. This calls for more love to cover a multitude of
sins, more grace for forgiveness, more of the Spirit's graces of
longsuffering and patience. But do not allow sin to get into your
marriage in the first place. Be jealous for your relationship's health
and beauty. Be slow to speak, as James says, and slow to be angry.
Be quick to forgive and quick to seek forgiveness. This is basic
Christian living.

Secondly, be zealous to be the kind of wife who is more con-
cerned with pleasing God than with being pleased by your husband. Sometimes, for one reason or another, Christian women
find themselves married to ungodly men. Of course, this is a
trial. However, a faithful Christian woman can make the circumstances much better by being obedient. A disobedient wife, on
the other hand, can always make things worse. This is one of my
husband's regular exhortations to couples in this type of situation:
Things may be bad now, but you can always make them a whole
lot worse. Unfortunately, they often do.

What does the Scripture teach? Are you respecting your husband? Are you seeking to honor and obey him? Or are you nit-
picking, backbiting, criticizing, complaining, and being generally
unpleasant? A wife can become so focused on her husband's sins
(and they *are* real), that she is blinded to her own. This is the time
to go back to the first things. Seek your husband's forgiveness for

running him down. Confess to the children your disrespect and disobedience to their father. Ask God to give you a clean heart and the grace and strength to obey Him.

God is faithful. He forgives and cleanses and strengthens. He has promised He will never leave us or forsake us. But we cannot lean on His promises if we are indulging a hard heart and living in disobedience to His simplest commands.

There is no way to begin untying the knots of your marriage if you are the central knot, and often this is the case. And just because a wife repents, that is no guarantee that her husband will follow suit and repent as well. But it does mean that the process can begin. If only one person begins to put things right, there is hope that the marriage can be saved. Why else would Scripture encourage women to win their husbands without a word (1 Pet. 3:1–6)? This passage implies two things: first, women are tempted to talk, talk, nag, nag; and second, husbands can be won. God uses a quiet wife to work in the heart of a disobedient husband. This is His ordained means.

We cannot expect God to fix our marriage problems and bring about resolutions to our difficulties if we are not willing to obey His every word. We cannot brush off verses about honor and respect and winning without a word, telling ourselves that they just don't apply in our case. This is foolishness. Get back to the basics. Don't indulge sin. Don't tolerate it in yourself. Obey God in the little things, and you won't be susceptible to big sins. In short, live like a Christian woman. Then you can ask Him to begin to untangle the mess of your marriage—but not before.

Part 4

Mothering

Family Stories

<><><><><><><><><><><><><><><><><><><><><><><><><><><><><><><><><><><><>

Though a family has many collective memories of travels and holidays, birthdays and games, a big chunk of the culture and history of the family is its stories. These may be stories of things that really happened, or made-up stories improvised at bedtime, or they may be the stories in books that were read around the table, on the couch, on the back porch, or out in the yard.

My children can't think of *Lorna Doone* without remembering the men's retreat at Star Ranch where I read it to them for hours on end while their father was teaching. I can't think of the *Chronicles of Narnia* or Tolkien's *Lord of the Rings* without seeing in my mind's eye the bright red-hot cheeks of my son while he listened intently to the battle scenes. I can still see three little kids lined up on top of their father while he was stretched out on the couch, reading, reading, reading. One summer he again read the whole Tolkien trilogy aloud to us, each night reading until he got hoarse. The kids just wouldn't let him stop. When we traveled to Nebraska for a family reunion, we listened to the audio version and had to portion them out carefully to make them last for the whole trip.

But we weren't completely stuck in Narnia and Middle Earth. When my daughter had a bout with late-night croup, we would read *Chatterer the Red Squirrel* while sitting on the dryer in the bathroom with the shower steaming. That squirrel is an important part of our history. We drank Coke, read, and steamed together until she could breathe well enough to go back to sleep. (I know,

I know: Why were we drinking Coke in the middle of the night? Because it was fun.)

We came to love the hilarious stories about Penrod and the great tar fight; we became fast friends with Bertie Wooster (and Uncle Fred); we laughed over the "first deer" as told by Patrick McManus. Now my husband reads those same short stories to the college students on Friday nights when they come over for an evening of fellowship, psalm singing, and readings. Every young person really must become acquainted with Penrod and Uncle Fred.

I think P. G. Wodehouse is probably responsible more than we know for the humor in *Credenda*. Too much Wodehouse gets a person to think a little sideways. It has certainly contributed to my own children's descriptions and storytelling. They couldn't go to the grocery store or mailbox without coming back with a story. I still remember the story of the man wearing a three-piece suit and a pair of old-fashioned roller skates who came flying down a very steep hill at full speed—holding his commuter coffee cup, no less—and screeched to an elegant stop at the traffic light at the bottom. I never saw the scene with my own eyes, but my children told me the story in elaborate detail.

Each night around the dinner table we were prepared to hear stories about school. The time Carl accidentally lit himself on fire; how Jamin's little brother jumped off the swing and broke both wrists; the time Nathan opened a locker to check on some noise and found a little boy "hiding from school"; the many bus breakdown episodes on the way to track meets. The list goes on and on. Stories surrounded my children on all sides, and they had to jostle and jockey to get to the front of the line to tell us their story. Sometimes my husband had to tell them what order to go in so they would calm down.

If you think about the guests you have had to your home, the most interesting ones are those who tell stories. Of course there were times we had to tell our kids to quiet down. But they have rescued us several times when we've had ultra-quiet guests. They can go on and on and recall with great detail all kinds of silly stories of things that have happened to them. And they can tell their favorites over and over. Once my daughter and I went to a social event that turned out to be much smaller than expected, and everyone there was very quiet. She told me later, "Mom, I felt it was one of those times when I just had to use my gifts." So she launched into telling stories and enlivened the whole place.

Now that they are not at my table every night, I have had to pick up the pace. I miss their storytelling. Now when they tell stories, it is about their own children—like the time Knox, age three, headed off to my house in the early morning hours, pulling Jemima (in her diaper) in the wagon. It must have been an angel that woke my daughter up with a start. She jumped out of bed, threw on her clothes on the way down the stairs, never even looking in the kids' bedroom, and flew out the door just in time to see them heading down the street!

The most embarrassing stories were the ones I made up at bedtime when my children were very small. Stupid really. But the kids loved them. They were usually about animals that could talk and very small little boys who lived in the trees. Their own storytelling surpassed mine long ago. And now I am telling those same silly stories to my grandchildren. But better yet, they are now telling me their own stories with wide eyes.

The Postpartum Mother

$$\diamond$$

Whenever I address a topic related to childbirthing, it is a very delicate operation indeed. Women have strong loyalties and views, as well as birth stories and experiences that may conflict with what I say, and I do not want to give offense needlessly. So in this article I hope to encourage and edify, not discourage or offend.

In all things related to pregnancy, childbirth, and the postpartum mother, a Christian woman is called to think and act like a Christian. In our day, as in every other generation, the secular community is eager to give its input and make disciples. Most modern books about pregnancy and childbirth espouse secular, non-Christian, and sometimes anti-Christian views. The Christian woman must gather her information with great care and wisdom as though she were picking flowers in a dangerous minefield.

Here are a few samples of such dangerous ideas:

- Often the pregnant woman is told to expect to be angry during birth. She will probably yell at her husband, and that is okay because labor pains are in fact painful.
- She may not even like her baby at first because of the trouble the child has caused her in birth.
- After the birth, she may experience depression for weeks.

Statements like this imply that a woman has no control over her own feelings and actions. What is wrong with this sort of preparation for childbirth and mothering? It can be frightening to a godly woman who fears she will be a disgrace to her God and her husband. Or it can give the weak Christian an excuse for all kinds of ungodly behavior. This mentality that makes provision for sin speaks nothing of duty and does not account at all for the promise of grace and strength from Christ.

Though many things relating to childbirth fall in the category of things indifferent, some items do not. What do I mean? Some matters are not moral issues, but wisdom issues. These include decisions like birthing at home versus the hospital, midwives versus doctors, pain medication versus an all-natural labor, breastfeeding versus the bottle, schedule feeding versus demand feeding. But some matters clearly are moral issues, and these include the demeanor of the new mother. Christian women (whether childbearing or not) are required to be patient in affliction, to cast their cares on the Lord, to trust Him in all their ways, and to honor and respect their husbands. These are moral issues that matter to God.

As the Christian woman approaches childbirth, she should endeavor to prepare herself spiritually as well as physically and mentally. She should pray that God would give her a gentle and quiet spirit as she enters into labor. She should seek to glorify God throughout the process, both in the preparation and the actual delivery. She should reject false ideas about her personality suddenly changing in labor, turning her into a sharp, nasty woman who is biting people's heads off. This is a lie. If she is normally quick to be angry, certainly labor will be just another opportunity to sin. But if she is normally a kind-hearted woman, she will continue to be so even under the provocation of labor.

The world wants to excuse sin and does so by calling things "syndromes." Childbirth is something women are equipped by God to do. He has promised to keep His people, and He will certainly not abandon His children at a moment when He is bringing a new covenant child into the world. "The eternal God is thy refuge, and underneath are the everlasting arms" (Deut. 33:27).

The everlasting arms are something a new mother can eternally trust. In this, as in everything, the Christian has a tremendous advantage over the unbeliever: the promises are ours! Christ will never leave us or forsake us. He wants to bless us and provide for us in all conditions. Our business is to rest in Him.

At the same time, we are flesh and blood. He knows our frame. We are not to see ourselves as cartoon bionic women who can do anything: "No drugs, no doctors, no problem!" We may become frightened. We may grow weary. We may wonder why we are shedding tears. We must remember that He is sanctifying us; we are all at different places in this supernatural process. So we must be kind to one another and bear one another's burdens. If a weaker sister "loses it" in childbirth, then we gently instruct her and forgive her and pray better things of her next time. If she becomes "depressed" after childbirth, we must seek to help her. It may be hormones. What isn't? It may be that she thinks she is expected to have a bout with the postpartum blues, and so she is doing her best to do what she has been told. She may not know what is causing it. But we must encourage her not to give way to it.

The blues are common, but we must not indulge ourselves in them. Yes, it is common for some women to feel blue after birth. For some it is a passing feeling that only lasts a few minutes. For others it may persist longer. And some cannot imagine feeling blue after such an exhilarating event. But for those who do lose heart, we must cheer them on. We must exhort them to resist the temptation to stop and analyze what is going on, falling into an endless cycle of introspection. Cast your cares upon God and then seek His strength to move on. There is too much work to be done!

Birthing is such a glorious privilege and high calling. We must embrace it with wisdom and hardheaded obedience. We ought to stay away from reading stupid stuff or listening to foolish women. We should determine before God, by the grace of God, to make our husbands proud of us as we do our hard work of bringing children into the world. We must not forget who we are or in Whom we trust. The eternal God is our refuge at all times, particularly as we fulfill our calling by bearing children.

Your Baby Has a Soul

◇◇

The Apostle John begins his third epistle with a wonderful greeting and prayer in verse three: "Beloved, I pray that you may prosper in all things and be in health, just as your soul prospers." John thought in terms of the souls of his loved ones. And the Old Testament is filled with warnings to "take heed to your soul." God wants us to pay attention to the state of our souls. We are responsible to see that our souls are prospering, taking root, and thriving like vigorous plants, not declining or drooping like wilted seedlings in the hot sun.

Not only that, but we are responsible to see that our children's souls are prospering as well. Parents are the means God has established to nurture these little souls, and mothers share this tremendous privilege and responsibility to see that, by God's grace, all the children in their charge are flourishing, both body and soul.

Many people in our modern soulless culture deny even the existence of the soul, much less consider the state of their own souls or the souls of their children. But we know better. Wise mothers should be tuned in to this crucial aspect of their mothering. Mothering is not just about childbirth options or schedule feeding. The wise woman understands that children are a source of joy and blessing entrusted to her by God, and she is to be a good steward of them, seeing that she takes care to dedicate her children to God and train them up as God's own.

When a new baby is in his mother's arms, we don't understand what God is doing to nurture the baby's wee soul. It is a mystery.

But He uses every loving word, every silly song, every kiss and playful hug to nurture and nourish the souls of our children. This is a work of faith, and we trust God to do it through us. Laying aside our own plans in order to rock a baby or comfort a child is a soul-prospering work, not an annoying interruption.

Though a mother's work can seem monotonous or repetitive when it comes to doing the laundry or changing the diapers, we have to have the eye of faith as we go. God blesses all these loving duties to the prospering of the souls of both mother and children. Reading stories over and over, stacking the blocks one more time, washing a face, wiping a nose, changing a wet diaper, or putting fresh sheets on the bed are all ways a mother cares for her children and communicates love and security. And in some mysterious way, God uses it like sunshine and water on a tender plant. So we plant and water, but He gives the increase.

All the loving attentiveness a mother gives her children is food for their souls. When the child is a small baby, all those smiles and kind words, the laughing and playfulness, and the motherly delight and pride in each new accomplishment is used by God to prosper the baby's soul. And it continues as the child grows. Even the smallest gesture, if done in love and kindness, is nourishing. We want our children to have fat little souls, to be healthy plants, as in Psalm 144:12: "that our sons may be as plants grown up in their youth." The child cannot find the same soul-nourishment from a stranger or casual acquaintance. That's why when a child is hurt, he always turns to his parents for comfort, no matter how nice the babysitter is. And that is a good sign, not a bad sign. Children find security in their own parents, and if they don't, then they will look elsewhere, even to strangers.

A child growing up in a home filled with selfishness, criticism, impatience, and bitterness does not flourish. How can he? His soul is malnourished, stunted, and neglected. Parents often do not take seriously the tremendous impact their lives have on their children. They fail to realize how potent their words and actions are, for good or ill. Mothers who hand off their babies, who are too busy for their children, or who grow impatient, cross, or scolding with the many demands on them are rearing unhealthy children. They are starving them spiritually. Sticking them in front of the television for hours is soul-deadening. Ignoring them when they ask questions, or telling them "I'm too busy right now," is like giving them a crust of bread for dinner. Nothing we do is neutral; it will either feed and nourish or starve and impoverish. We cannot think that a prayer at bedtime and reading a Bible story to them occasionally will counteract the damage done day in and day out by the foul air the children breathe in the home day after day all year long. This kind of mother is tearing her house down with her own hands (and her own tongue).

The mother is designed by God to be a source of great blessing to her husband and children; she is to be the "very soul of the house." And mothers underestimate the power in their hands to bring their families great good. As Proverbs says, "Better is a dinner of herbs where love is, than a fatted calf with hatred" (15:17), and "Better is a dry morsel with quietness, than a house full of feasting with strife" (17:1). Note, though, that those are not the only two options. By the grace of God, mothers can provide peaceful and joyful feasts which nourish both body and soul. Listening to your children, taking them on your lap and talking with them, and being affectionate and loving to them will of course take time. Just as preparing and serving good food takes time, so feeding our children's souls takes time. Though we cannot see the food doing its work at the table, we do see our children growing over time. The same is true of nourishing their souls. We cannot see how reading this story one more time will be like a second helping of mashed potatoes, but it is. God uses all these things we do, when we render them unto Him by faith, to strengthen, nourish, and grow our children up into men and women with fat souls who will then be able to nourish their own children and grandchildren.

Mothers and Sons

◇◇◇

David is singing praise to God in Psalm 144, praying for deliverance from his enemies, seeking God's continued blessing on His people, and describing what he envisions this blessing will look like. Part of this description is verse twelve: "That our sons may be as plants grown up in their youth." Sons who are blessed of God are likened to plants that achieve maturity while they are still young. A plant grown up in its youth is a picture not only of early maturity, but also of significance, productivity, and strength. This kind of son is impressive in stature, despite his youth.

Though we acknowledge with David that God is the One who is the source of such blessing, we also realize that He uses means to accomplish His ends. And mothers are one of these ordained means. Mothers have the opportunity to bring great good to their sons, but they can also enfeeble them. Let's consider a few things mothers can do, and a few things they should avoid doing, as they bring their sons up in the Lord.

First things should always come first. A mother must be a faithful Christian and a faithful wife before she can fulfill her secondary duties as a mother. One of the best things a mother can do for her son is to demonstrate to him that she takes the Bible seriously by walking in obedience to God and respecting her husband, her son's father. A boy finds joy in seeing his father respected. This is the way God has made sons.

Sons run on respect just like their fathers, and it is important that they not only see their fathers respected, but they must receive respect in the home as well. It will look different from the respect that the head of the house receives, but sons need to be praised and admired for their achievements and accomplishments just like Dad. This means mothers treat their sons with courtesy, and sisters are taught to treat their brothers the same way. Courtesy excludes scolding, running down, picking on, or criticizing. Mothers should not share their son's weaknesses, failures, or sins any more than they should share their husband's. Rather, they should seek to build them up, encourage them, and praise them for their good work.

The mama-bear syndrome does not encourage masculinity. The mama-bear is the mother who wants to fight all her son's battles for him and pick up all the pieces when he fails. This kind of mother shoulders all her son's responsibility for him and teaches him to look for a wife who will continue to mother him in this way.

Sons need to be given responsibility suited to their age and gifts. This might mean helping to look after little sister or setting the table when they are young. But their responsibilities should take on more size and significance as they get bigger. Because sons should not be taught to be home-centered like their sisters, they need to learn masculine tasks. This does not mean sons cannot help in the kitchen, but it does mean they should be taught that the kitchen is not their long-term destination. They will find their calling outside the home.

Mothers need to require both physical and mental toughness from their sons. Though motherly affection is a godly attribute, it can run amok when it turns into sentimental mollycoddling and indulgence. Physical toughness means sons have to learn to suck it up. When a toddler falls down and skins his knee, of course a hug and a kiss from Mom is essential. But then he must be told when the crying should be all done. A few seconds may be plenty, depending on how severe the injury. But there is no need to let it drag out. Take a breath. Be tough. All done.

If a toddler is allowed to become hysterical when he gets hurt, it will take him far more effort to learn to control himself later. Mothers especially need to be taught to be tough for and with their sons. If a junior-high-age son is still crying when he gets hurt, something is seriously amiss. But self-control includes temper as well. A son who doesn't cry but yells and stomps is just as much an embarrassment as the son who bawls. Neither behavior should be tolerated in sons.

This goes for academics as well. It does not matter whether Mom is backing up a teacher or if she is the teacher herself—sons must be held to high standards. Academic laziness is as deadly as physical laziness. Sons must be required to work hard in both areas, and they must suffer the consequences when they slack off. This means that mothers must not give in to excuses. Just because a son does not like math or does not show an aptitude for reading does not mean he should be allowed to skip it this year. That is a grievous mistake that will teach him he doesn't have to exert himself in areas that are unappealing to him. Far from equipping a young man to be a leader, this kind of limpness emasculates sons.

As we bring up sons before the Lord, all our training and teaching must be saturated with Scripture. We cannot expect our sons to be mature without filling them with much biblical teaching. Every mother should give her son the book of Proverbs to read and reread. He must be taught that he is expected to do these things because He serves a good and holy God. This, by God's grace, will equip and prepare our sons to take their places in the city gates with their fathers.

Mothers and Daughters

I love the beautiful expression in Psalm 144:12 describing covenant daughters in a culture blessed by God: "that our daughters may be as corner stones, polished after the similitude of a palace." What a wonderful way to think of our daughters!

The cornerstone is a very significant, impressive part of the building, and vital to the foundation. But this psalm is not describing the cornerstone of any old building—it is the polished marble of a palace. When God is blessing His people, covenant daughters are refined, intelligent, beautiful, and noble. Their contribution to the culture both supports and adorns—they bear much weight and responsibility with the loveliness that comes of grace, discipline, and dignity.

If we desire to see God bless us with such daughters, we must first compare our own view with that of Scripture. I am afraid that sometimes daughters are viewed as second-class citizens, not being educated as well as the sons, and not being prepared to take their position as polished cornerstones. As we respond to the rampant feminism and egalitarianism in our day, we must not overreact by neglecting the serious task of preparing young women for all God is calling them to. When our culture is truly blessed of God, our daughters will be something to behold. Of course, getting there will take wisdom, but God promises to give it to us when we ask in faith.

How can mothers help nurture their daughters to the stature of polished cornerstones? The first thing is to cultivate a high view of what it takes to be a wife and mother. This includes having high standards of academic work for daughters as well as sons. If all that is expected of daughters is basic literacy so they can read a cookbook, we are falling tremendously short. Homemaking requires far more than this, and it will be much more satisfying to the woman who understands the momentousness of her task.

Because we have embraced the biblical view of children (blessed is the man whose quiver is full), many women have found themselves in a home with a very large family. This can be a great blessing, or it can be a spectacular failure. If it really is a blessing, then daughters from such families will want the same for themselves.

But all too often older daughters can hardly wait to be away from home because they are carrying so much of Mom's responsibility of childrearing, homeschooling, and babysitting. Some of these daughters leave home hostile to the idea of a large family. They have seen what a drag and weight it has been on both their mothers and themselves, and they want no part of carrying on such a tradition.

This attitude can result from mothers viewing their older daughters as full-time babysitters. These girls often cannot pursue academics because they are busy teaching the little ones, so their own progress is stunted. They have become surrogate mothers whose days are full of diapers and cooking and cleaning, and though they are becoming proficient in domestic duties, they must of necessity neglect intellectual pursuits. For daughters to assume their rightful role in the covenant community, they must be proficient in both. We are shortsighted if we think we can raise up sons to be great leaders, embracing a biblical masculinity, while raising up enfeebled women to be their helpers.

God has created our daughters to need love and security. When parents love their daughters, they are bestowing protection and security on them, and this in turn keeps them from looking for affirmation elsewhere. A daughter who is loved will be lovely. She won't be competing for attention from unsuitable guys; she won't be insecure about who she is and what she is supposed to be doing. Women need protection from men, and parents (particularly dads) are designated to protect their daughters until such time that they are given in marriage to husbands who will take up this duty of protecting.

Loving daughters means providing a full-orbed education for them. It means providing for all their needs. Daughters need to be adorned physically, which means teaching them to be lovely, and teaching them how to shop and sew. It means teaching them to have good taste and to appreciate lovely things. A polished cornerstone implies refinement and beauty and virtue. This means we do not confuse modest with frumpy. Covering our daughters in second-hand, neck-to-ankle jumpers that are two sizes too big is not teaching a feminine, modest beauty. We must learn what beauty is ourselves and then adorn our daughters appropriately and modestly.

Finally, mothers must not be critical of their daughters. A godly discipline will not allow silliness, idleness, bossiness, shyness, poutiness, or other forms of manipulation. But at the same time, a loving mother will not nitpick, criticize, attribute motives, take things personally, or be demanding and hard on daughters. Remember, daughters need love and security. A critical, unforgiving spirit will alienate a daughter very fast. Mothers must keep their perspective in this and let love cover a multitude of sins.

Daughters will sin like everyone else. Mothers must model forgiveness and repentance by seeking it themselves when they have been too hard on them. Then, by the grace of God, covenant daughters will delight in their mothers, and mothers will rejoice to see their daughters taking their places as polished cornerstones.

Sons and Sports

◇◇

Yes, you read the title right. I really am writing about why sons should be in sports. And, yes, this is a topic for wives and mothers, not for husbands and dads. I feel qualified to address this subject because I put in hundreds (I'm not exaggerating) of hours in the bleachers. Soccer, T-ball, baseball, lacrosse, basketball, track, football (did I forget anything?)— my son did them all. (And I'm not including my daughter's track, basketball, and volleyball here. That will come up another time.) And I might as well mention it here: Invest in one of those little cushy seats to take with you to all the games. Bleachers are very uncomfortable.

Call me a cheerleader if you will (though I never had pom-poms), but I am one of those moms who is a strong proponent of boys in sports. Why? Because it is good for them. Sports can teach boys important things that Mom cannot teach them. And moms can learn a thing or two about their sons by having them involved in sports.

But some moms are jumpy about their sons being in sports. It doesn't seem very spiritual for them to be tackling someone, or stealing a ball or a base, or hitting an opponent (or being hit) with a lacrosse stick. In fact, it doesn't sound very spiritual to have an opponent!

Let's think about these things. I'm going to give you three (or four) good reasons for your boys to be involved in sports. I'm sure there are many more reasons, but this is a brief essay, so I will lay out my own motherly thoughts on the subject.

First of all, the way I see it, boys need to learn how to take a hit. Christian men need to be fighters. After all, in Christendom there is a battle going on. Young boys need to be trained in many areas beyond academics if they are going to be skilled in battle. For starters, they need to be tough—not whiners, moaners, wimps, or shirkers. In sports they learn to take a hit. And I learned how to take a hit from my vantage point in the bleachers when my son took a hit. (Third down and thirty-five against the defending state champions. Screen pass. He met three defenders at the marker. Went on top, through the crowd cable, and into and under the bleachers.)

We do not want the church populated with men who cry when they fall down. If they are pushed around on the basketball court, they will learn how to "suck it up" and "blow it out," as my son-in-law says. When they look at the gigantic size of the other team and see how completely understaffed they are, they will find courage to overcome. Men need to be protectors and fighters. Sports are a good way to introduce them to the idea. It is not a real war, but it is good training for the real ones.

Second, competing in sports requires discipline, and discipline is good. Boys need to run and run and run until they don't think they can run anymore, and then they need to run some more. This is why it is such a blessing to have a coach who thinks boys need to do this. If a coach allows them to take a little breather if their side hurts, they won't do so well in the world of real fighting. A good and godly coach is a huge blessing.

Moms don't make good coaches for sons (although I know there are exceptions to this) because they want to have cookie-and-milk breaks, and they want to call the boys inside when it starts to rain. (We make far better cheerleaders and far better cookies.)

My son had to get up early to make it to 6 a.m. basketball practice every morning in the dead of winter when it was cold and very dark. He was tired when he went to bed at night. He had two-a-days in football in the heat of August, and he slept very well. He had to learn to do what his coach told him to do, no matter what he thought of it. This is a good lesson for a son to learn. Sports teach sons the discipline of obeying authority and pushing their bodies to do what they are told even when those bodies are tired.

But sports do more than this. They also teach sons how to work with a team, how to submit to authority, how to encourage the slow guy, how to hit hard. And they teach patience. Time on the bench can be sanctifying, teaching humility and endurance—just so long as the time on the bench is not for poor conduct. But that can be a lesson also. I love a coach who will not stand for any slackness. I love a coach who calls a player to the bench who is not doing what he is told. I love a coach who will not let a kid play who was late for practice or who was showboating on the court.

Sports are also very revealing. You see how your son is doing spiritually. And you see how you are doing spiritually. Is he throwing a tantrum when he doesn't get to play? Are you? Is he a crummy loser? Are you? Is he crying when he falls down? Are you? Is he kicking the ball in anger when he misses a shot? Is he passing the ball on the court or is he trying to get all the points himself? Is he playing dirty or giving the ref a bad time? Sports can show you all too plainly where your son's weak points really are, in front of you and everybody.

Finally, sports can give your son something to be proud of and something for you to be proud of as well. That's right. There can be a godly satisfaction and delight in catching the fly ball, in passing the scoring touchdown, and in running a really good race. This is the way God made us.

And one last thing. Moms, don't treat your sons like they are daughters. I am with you when you say you don't want your girls playing football. But a son is a totally different animal. Overprotective mothers can end up destroying their sons. We want our sons to be tough and strong and able to handle heavy weather without being snapped in two. If we keep them in the temperature-regulated greenhouse of home, they will not mature to be like "plants grown up in their youth" (Ps. 144:12).

Daughters and Sports

It is all fine and good for sons to be subjected to the discipline and competition of sports, but what about our daughters? Is it healthy for them to be competing? I think it all depends.

We are not raising our daughters to be "fighters" the same way we are with our sons. At the same time, self-discipline and godly determination are great qualities for women to have. Daughters can learn a lot from sports. They can benefit from learning to push themselves, to work hard, and to be part of a team. Besides, physical activity has benefits for everyone. Women can enjoy the thrill of the race or the game like anyone else. Still, we have to look at sports for our daughters a little differently than we do for our sons.

The goal we have in mind in raising sons is to inculcate masculinity. And we want our daughters to embrace a godly femininity, not a worldly feminism. So when parents consider sports for their daughters, they ought to be thinking about whether her participation will help develop or hinder her.

Some sports are so completely masculine that young women shouldn't even think about participating. These certainly include football, boxing, and hockey. And it is just plain pitiful to see a woman force herself onto a male team just to cause a stink and force the boys to play with her. This is just a sad attempt for attention. Once when my son played football for a government high school (while he attended a local Christian school), the other team had a girl suited up and standing on the sidelines. My husband told my son, "If she gets out on the field, don't go near her, and don't tackle her. Just stand out of her way." Tackling is no way to treat a lady, even if she is refusing to act like one.

But the next important thing to consider is what kind of program is available. For example, volleyball can be a great sport for girls. But if the program is bent on treating the girls like they are boys, and they are encouraging the girls to act like boys, then I wouldn't want my daughters participating. But if the coaches are teaching the girls to play well and play like ladies, it can be a great experience. The same is true of basketball, softball, soccer, or track. If the girls are trying to act tough and masculine, it is deadly. But if they are enjoying the game and learning to work as a team, this can be working with the grain, teaching them to be feminine and beautiful as they handle the ball or hit it over the net. When our daughter played basketball for her Christian school, the team all wore blue ribbons in their hair as a feminine statement that they were not trying to act or look or play like boys. And they were a good team. They didn't trash talk or play dirty. They were taught to play like Christian women.

So if the sport itself is not masculine in nature, and if the program is deliberately striving to promote feminine virtue, then it can be a great blessing to young girls. But there are still pitfalls. Boys need to get hit and learn to take it, but girls need security and love. When insecure girls play sports, they are more susceptible to the temptations to try to become masculine. They may be looking for attention and affirmation from the sport when they really need it from their dads and their moms. They may "feel" unfeminine, so they gravitate to sports where they don't have to be feminine. This means that wise parents will closely monitor their daughters while they participate in sports. And if they begin to show signs of becoming "macho" or unfeminine, they should consider pulling them out.

I have seen the discipline of sports teach girls to be better stewards of their time, thus causing their studies to improve. Some exposure to sports can give our daughters confidence and make them "well-rounded" in their education. My daughter especially recommends volleyball for Christian girls because it is a team sport that can include lots of people, of all ages, and it is a great activity for church picnics.

And team sports are revealing when it comes to testing a daughter's character. She has to think fast, look out for others, follow directions, and develop skill. This is all good, and none of this is contrary to a biblical femininity.

Of course I have to say something about uniforms and modesty. Christians ought to insist on dressing modestly. That means daughters shouldn't be wearing tank tops with huge armholes and sports bras underneath. Neither should they be wearing what are called butt-huggers. It doesn't matter if the other team is wearing skimpy outfits. Christians ought to refuse to participate in a sport where they will have to compromise in this area. A girls' team can be dressed appropriately and modestly, even if it is no longer "cool" to do so. And this doesn't mean wearing knee-length culottes, or any length culottes, for that matter.

Volleyball and track teams are now wearing virtual swimsuits as uniforms, and it just isn't necessary. You can't tell me they really can play better or run faster in less clothing. It's about making the slower women's sports more interesting to watch. Male volleyball players don't seem too hampered by actual shorts.

Sports are not bad in themselves, but bad coaches can make for a miserable experience. If your daughter is in a sport, know the coaches, be at the games, and know how your daughter is doing. She certainly shouldn't be forced into playing a sport if she isn't inclined to do so. But if she wants to play, parents ought not to hinder her for the wrong reasons.

The Tomboy

From time to time I hear parents refer to a daughter as a tomboy. They may say it with a bit of parental pride or with a tone of grave concern. Either way, the term *tomboy* can encompass many things. To one mom it may mean her daughter loves to ride her bicycle and play outside. She may hate fussy, fluffy dresses, and she may dislike dolls altogether. But to another mom the term may mean her daughter wants to wear camouflage pants and combat boots to church and dreams of growing up to be a soldier. Obviously, these are very different. And of course there are all kinds of variations in between. What kinds of behavior should be alarming to a Christian parent? What sort of "tomboyish" behavior should be of no concern?

In both the dictionaries I consulted, a tomboy refers to a boisterous girl who is behaving like a boisterous boy—*boisterous* meaning loud, rough, and good-natured. There is only one thing worse than a swaggering, loud-mouthed boy, and that is a swaggering, loud-mouthed girl, good-natured or not. Though we do want our daughters to be cheerful, we would rather not encourage them to be loud and rough, taking on spitting and belching as though these were admirable traits. In fact, Scripture exhorts women to be sober-minded and modest, two virtues that seem to be at odds with loud and rough behavior.

But let's think about some of the more typical behavior that makes parents think they have a tomboy on their hands. First of all, having a daughter who loves to be outdoors is not necessarily at odds with her femininity, unless she wants to be a logger or a roofer. A woman can be a skilled horseback rider, archer, or shooter, but she should not go off to war. It is a mother's duty to steer such things, teaching her daughters that God requires husbands and fathers to go to war, not daughters and mothers.

In our so-called politically correct society, it is essential that we train our children to think biblically and to laugh out loud at the modern absurdities regarding gender roles. God has made Himself abundantly clear regarding our role assignments, and it is our duty to teach our children how to enjoy themselves as His obedient creatures in this as in every other area. Daughters must be taught to have real reverence and admiration for the high calling women have been given by God to be homemakers and life-givers. The central way to impart this is by esteeming our own calling in the home as wives and mothers.

Sometimes parents press a child into the tomboy mold. This may come about because a mother has trouble relating to a daughter because she does not seem very feminine in her appearance or interests. In that case, she may be dubbed a tomboy. Her parents may tell her regularly that she is a tomboy, and so she will simply strive to live up to the expectation. If she is not built like a china-doll, and her sisters or friends are, she may hear comparisons way too often. "Oh, she is our little tomboy, while little sister Susie here is so feminine and pretty!" It would be much wiser to teach, instruct, and encourage the naturally unfeminine one to be more feminine rather than reinforce her identity as a tomboy. (And, of course, the daughter who is overly given to fluffy dresses may need a little parental guidance in the other direction.)

For example, when a daughter first pronounces that she will not wear a dress, her mother should laugh and gently instruct her otherwise. If she begins to wear a baseball cap constantly, her parents should insist it come off. But this should have happened long before she turned fifteen. By that time it is very difficult to turn things around.

A girl who has been treated like a tomboy by her family may think her only future is in sports. And if she feels she cannot compete with the other girls in her looks, she may just give up all together and begin to adopt a more unfeminine persona as an attempt to say to everyone, "I don't care if you don't think I'm feminine, because I beat you to it: I don't want to be." This sort of daughter begins wearing dumpy, unfeminine clothes and doesn't make an effort to look lovely. This may annoy a mother, which just causes her to become more critical of her daughter: "Why can't you wear a dress like the other girls? Why can't you try to look a little more feminine like your sister?" And that will only alienate the daughter all the more, increasing her insecurity, and making her more unattractive.

Unfortunately, mothers can reinforce this by sins of omission as well: Not teaching their daughters how to do their hair or makeup, not encouraging them to be comfortable with their looks or shape, not complimenting them when they look good, not buying them attractive clothes or teaching them to love the lovely. And it's no good saying, "I don't know how to do hair or makeup, so I can't teach my daughter." You'd better learn how, and quick, or get out you wallet so someone else can help.

Finally, dads need to act. Mothers need to help spot these things early on and enlist Dad's aid in promoting, encouraging, and supporting (financially) femininity. This does not mean going overboard on the ruffles, but rather delighting in the way God has made us male and female and not blurring the distinctions.

Sons and Flattery

◇◇

Proverbs is full of admonitions to young men to stay far away from the strange woman, "for her house inclineth unto death, and her paths unto the dead" (Prov. 2:18). "Her end is bitter as wormwood, sharp as a two-edged sword. Her feet go down to death; her steps take hold on hell" (5:4). "None that go unto her return again, neither take they hold of the paths of life" (2:19). "But whoso committeth adultery with a woman lacketh understanding: he that doeth it destroyeth his own soul" (6:32). "For she hath cast down many wounded: yea, many strong men have been slain by her. Her house is the way to hell, going down to the chambers of death" (7:26–27). And finally, "The mouth of a strange woman is a deep pit: he that is abhorred of the Lord shall fall therein" (22:14).

Now given such manifold and dire warnings, whatever would possess a young man to turn aside to go after such a woman? What exactly is the pull? What is it that first lures him away to lust after her? Proverbs makes it very clear that the initial pull comes from flattery. The harlot practices her art on the "man void of understanding" (7:7); she "flattereth with her words" (7:5). "For the lips of a strange woman drop as an honeycomb, and her mouth is smoother than oil" (5:3). Godly instruction is offered to the young man for this purpose: "To deliver thee from the strange woman, even from the stranger which flattereth with her words"(2:16); "To keep thee from the evil woman, from the flattery of the tongue of a strange woman" (6:24).

From all this, it must be safe to assert that young men in particular are very vulnerable to flattery. This must be connected to their God-given need for respect and admiration; so it follows that a man who does not feel respected for his legitimate attributes will be a sitting duck for flattery. A hollow and shallow counterfeit for respect, flattery is marked by its insincerity and its excessiveness. The flatterer (in this case a woman) makes much of a man with the intent of ingratiating herself. She compliments him either by bestowing too much attention on him (hanging on his every word), by acting very impressed with him (or his car), or by saying stupid and untrue things to him. This may seem so obviously fake and phony to the one standing by watching, but to the poor stupid young man, it is wonderful.

So what is my point of application for women in this observation about men and flattery? I have several. The first is to wives: Respect your husband genuinely. This is obedience to God's Word, and it has a tremendous impact on your husband, not the least of which is the protection it provides him from the strange woman and her smooth speech. Men who have a "full tank" when it comes to respect from their own wives are far less vulnerable to the flattery of the strange woman.

But a second point of application is this: Wives, notice how the harlot knows what a man wants. She has made plans. She tells him she has decked out her bed and perfumed it as well (7:16–17). "With her much fair speech she caused him to yield, with the flattering of her lips she forced him. He goeth after her straightway, as an ox goeth to the slaughter" (7:21–22a). How much more protected would a man be if his own wife spoke to him like this? But in the wife's case, her words would not lead him to death, but rather to the marriage bed, honored by God. Wives could learn a thing or two from this harlot in Proverbs.

The next application is to moms: Respect your sons. A son runs on respect, just like his dad does. Instruction, teaching, admonition, and more instruction from Mom will not have the effect it should unless it is accompanied by respect. And what is respect?

Courtesy, kindness, giving responsibility, and providing account-ability, all within a framework of admiration and honor, humility and deference. Sons who have moms with this sort of perspective will not so easily fall prey to the silly talk of the airheaded girl in the tight T-shirt because he has been better equipped to discern the difference between flattery and real respect.

Proverbs is solid proof that young men need instruction from both their parents, but they need a good example to accompany the teaching. Instruction given this way will make a son grateful, not bitter. The strange woman is a serious threat. Godly instruc-tion prepares your son and equips him to stay away from her.

Finally, train and love your daughters so that they become wise women, not flirty, flighty girls looking for attention from the boys and willing to act foolishly to get it. What is flirting but just a milder form of flattery? But if it is indulged, it leads to the same end. Girls who are too interested in the boys and too quick to give the boys their full attention are obviously running on fumes. They are easy for the boys to impress. These girls are in great need of love and security, and if their dads don't provide it, they will look to the boys. And we all know that the boys will not really bring the needed security but will only increase the in-security. The strange woman in Proverbs has refined her art and made her insecurity into a commodity she can sell. And there is always a market.

Part 5

Attitudes

Pursuing Virtue

◇◇◇

And now, my daughter, fear not; I will do to thee all that thou requirest: for all the city of my people doth know that thou art a virtuous woman" (Ruth 3:11). Ruth was known throughout her community as a *virtuous* woman. This is rather an archaic term for us today because few people even have a category for virtue. If you take a walk through a department store, especially through the junior section that caters to teenagers, you will see that virtue is indeed out of fashion.

The reason many young women dress like prostitutes today is simple: It's what is in style. Short skirts with slits that go up way too high, tight T-shirts that stop several inches too short (to be worn with pants that begin way too low, flashing belly and back). And shirts worn too tight, too low, half unbuttoned on the top, and half unbuttoned on the bottom, making us wonder what the buttons are for anyway.

Tastelessness has become an art form. The last thing women in America today want to be known for is *virtue*. How stupid to be thought a virgin—or worse, to look like one. But this is the way the world always has been, and it should really not be such a surprise to us.

Isaiah describes the haughty daughters of Zion (chap. 3) who flaunt themselves in similar ways. What should surprise us is when the Christian sisters imitate the stupidity of the world. Christian women, of all women on earth, ought to think and dress and act in a manner that is completely contrary to the world. Paul tells us

(Rom. 12:2) not to be conformed to this world but to be trans-
formed by the renewing of our minds. Virtue for us should be a
delight to think about, to strive for, and to lay hold of. We should
long to identify with Ruth and be the kind of women who are
known in our families and in our communities as virtuous.

What does it mean to be a virtuous woman today? Though
times may change, God's Word does not, so it means the same
today as it did in Ruth's day. Being virtuous is being holy, righteous, upright, and pure. We are declared righteous in Christ, and
we are given virtue in our justification: "For he hath made him
to be sin for us, who knew no sin; that we might be made the
righteousness of God in him" (2 Cor. 5:21). Christ's excellence
and virtue and perfection are exchanged for our sinfulness, and
we are made righteous in Him. This is the gift we receive in our
justification. We are perfect in Christ because Christ is perfect,
not because we are.

Our sanctification, being an ongoing process fitting us for
heaven, requires our diligence, by means of the Holy Spirit, in
pursuing righteousness in our thoughts, our speech, and our lives.
A virtuous woman is one who is known in the Christian community for her high moral standard; she believes the Bible and
applies it to herself. She does not cut corners, make exceptions, or
excuse sinful behavior.

Ruth could have left Naomi for her own people who did not
fear God, but she chose to stay with her mother-in-law, which
meant following Naomi's God. A virtuous woman leaves the
world to follow after Christ, even if it means leaving the good
opinion of family and friends.

A virtuous woman is eager to be taught God's Word, to learn
wisdom, and to apply all she learns. She wants to know, she wants
to be virtuous because it is the means of glorifying God. So a virtuous woman is a learner and a doer. It is not enough, James tells
us, to be hearers only. Paul prays the Colossians (1:10) will "walk
worthy of the Lord unto all pleasing, being fruitful in every good
work, and increasing in the knowledge of God." This increase of

knowledge comes passively as she receives godly instruction, but also actively as she walks in the good works God has prepared for her. This is being fruitful, which also increases knowledge.

Walking worthy entails the high moral standard mentioned above. It means governing what we listen to, watch, or read, "denying ungodliness and worldy lusts" (Titus 2:12). This may include denying ourselves things we have come to enjoy very much. Where there has been compromise and slackness, it must be replaced with repentance and diligence. We cannot expect to walk worthy and be known for our virtue if we are filling our thoughts and time with ungodly and impure entertainments. We may have to deny such things verbally to friends who want us to listen to stupid music, read unchaste magazines, or watch immoral movies.

Living and walking worthy of Christ means dressing in modest, chaste clothing that is consistent with a life of virtue and godliness. This requires wisdom, and most young women don't want to exercise wisdom in this area. They care more about attracting attention from the young men than they care about pleasing God. Walking worthy means our behavior is governed by a desire to glorify God and obey Him in all things. It means actively pursuing virtue, not coasting. If we want to glorify God as His servants, and be known in our community as virtuous women, we must embrace God's standard of holiness in every area of our lives and reject every worldly standard that conflicts with this. Ruth was a relatively young woman when she was praised this way by Boaz. Young women need not think this is something for them to think about later. It is essential now.

Chick Flicks

◇◇

God created men and women with many differences, and one of the significant differences is how we are wired sexually. So, of course, given our differences, our temptations are not the same. The enemy of our souls, being an experienced strategist, hits us where we are weak.

Generally speaking, men are aroused by sight and are wired to their appetites, and so we have the porn industry working hard night and day to devise ways to devour and destroy men. Millions of men have been seduced, captured, and made slaves, all the while thinking they are exercising their "freedom." The attack is straightforward, in your face, and with no subtlety at all.

Women, on the other hand, generally speaking, are seduced emotionally and perhaps more subtly. Women are wired to their emotions and respond to touch, as well as to tenderness, thoughtfulness, sacrifice, and sentiment. Thus we have an industry devoted to producing sappy romantic novels, hours of TV time filled with soap operas, and films that aim to seduce women by drawing them into a vicarious illicit relationship.

In drawing these distinctions between men and women, I am not saying that either set of strengths/weaknesses necessitates falling into sin. And I am certainly not saying that women cannot be seduced by sight or men by tenderness. These categories are generalizations. Still, if we are going to understand how to resist our own temptations, we must be acquainted with our vulnerabilities.

One genre of film that has achieved popularity in recent years among women is what is commonly called the "chick flick." This is the movie that revolves around a relationship; it satisfies the emotional feminine need for masculine understanding and tenderness and has a happy ending culminating in a successful relationship. Now of course not all chick flicks are necessarily bad. But it is helpful if women understand what is going on in these stories, and it is crucial that we see what effect they are having on the women who watch them. And of course romantic novels present the same temptations as romantic films.

A chick flick may be great art, like some adaptations of *Pride and Prejudice*, or it may be altogether poor, like so many movies that come and go. Just because it is a story geared for women does not mean it is necessarily evil; women must guard themselves no matter what they are reading or watching. I am addressing here a particular temptation involving romantic works of fiction or film.

If watching or reading *Pride and Prejudice* causes a woman to become discontented with her own husband because he just doesn't match up to Mr. Darcy, then she is not reading cautiously. Works of fiction (including film) should delight and instruct us, not cause us to get into sin. If they do, either they are not worthy of our time, or we are not thinking properly when we watch or read them. Let's consider each of these categories separately.

In *The Discarded Image*, C. S. Lewis pointed out three essential tests of literature: It should teach what is useful, honor what is honorable, and appreciate the delightful. If a book or film is teaching destructive philosophy, if it is honoring fornication or adultery, if it is appreciating what is reprehensible, then we can safely conclude that this is not what we should find amusing or entertaining. A film that elevates adultery and leads us to sympathize with sin cannot be good for our souls. The romantic hero is often rebellious, individualistic, and guided by his passions. Women who are sucked into reading book after book with this kind of hero are going to be affected in an unhealthy way.

On the other hand, even if a film or book is first-rate, we still have to be thinking as we read or watch it. Even the good stuff can cause us to stumble, and we need to be paying attention. Guard against fantasizing about other men, even if they are just from the pages of a book. Both the married and the unmarried woman need to consider this. Some have called the emotional, romantic film "feminine porn"—it can seduce women into approving of ungodly conduct and relations. It can arouse the passions in an ungodly way, encouraging women to fantasize about men who are not their husbands, or lead to unhealthy mental role-playing. Unmarried women can be misled into thinking this is what a loving relationship is like. Married women can become discontented that they are not lusted for, sought, and chased after like the women in the book or film.

Women are led into lust in a different way than men are. Women lust to be lusted after, and seeing a film or reading a book that arouses this kind of lust can be very destructive. Though a woman may not be aroused at the sight of another woman taking off her clothes, it can make her wish she could do that, or look like that, or get men to look at her that way. This is clearly sinful thinking that needs to be repented of and forsaken, and it cannot be justified by saying, "But I am imagining seducing my husband like that woman on the screen."

Women may think when a "bad skin scene" comes on that only the men should turn their heads. But this is indeed a double standard. Women can be tripped up by such scenes as well, even though it represents a different form of lust. Such lust can lead to discontentment in her own relationship, and a little discontent can lead to a host of other sins.

A steady diet of romantic novels and films can have a devastating effect on the home. Women can begin to look to their books for fulfillment instead of to their husbands. They can view their own relationship in terms of their "unmet needs" and view their husbands as falling far short of the romantic ideal. This can lead over time to the desire to find a new, "satisfying" relationship where someone will sweep her off her feet and carry her away to a world where there are no responsibilities, only passion.

A good dose of biblical thinking is the best way to counter romanticism of this kind. God wants us to honor Him in our long-term relationships that are hedged in by His covenant of love. We are not to live for the moment, from one emotional high to another. And He knows what is good for our souls.

Contentious Women

◇◇◇

Everyone wants a pleasant home. And it's probably safe to say that nobody wants to live in a miserable, unhappy place. But it's very clear that a pleasant home is not something that can be bought with cash. If that were the case, rich people would be happy, and we all know that very few of them are.

What is it that makes our homes truly pleasant places? Without a doubt, it is godly wisdom. When wisdom is at home, home is a delight. So it follows that a pleasant home is one that has a wise, virtuous woman in the center of it. Proverbs has many vivid descriptions of the wise woman and the foolish woman. For starters, consider Proverbs 14:1: "Every wise woman buildeth her house, but the foolish plucketh it down with her hands." Both these women are busy, and their behavior has a considerable impact on their homes and families. But the wise woman is constructing, while the foolish woman is destructing. We could argue that at least the foolish woman is home-centered. Sure she is. The same way a demolition crew is home-centered when it aims the wrecking ball. The home is a sad target, and what a tragedy it is when the person designed by God to be one of the chief blessings becomes instead a shame and a destroyer.

Charles Bridges, a pastor from the late nineteenth century, says in his commentary on Proverbs, "Many are the miseries of a man's life; but none like that which cometh from one who should be the stay of his life." He goes on to say that a contentious wife is a great domestic calamity, and there is no lawful escape. A rebellious son can at least be thrown out of the house, he says, but a bad wife must simply be endured.

The book of Proverbs backs this up. A brawling, contentious, quarrelsome, indiscreet, ignorant woman is a great affliction to her husband and family. It would be better to sleep on the roof, or in the desert, than to endure her anger and bitterness. Solomon says it would be better to face rough weather than deal with her. After all, in this case, the weather may be worse inside than it is out. A man is better off alone than living with a woman like this.

Most Christian women readily assume they are not in this category of "brawling and contentious." But I would like to fine-tune this concern a little so we can all take heed. I've seen women destroy their homes, and it usually didn't happen in a day. It was years of nagging, complaining, discontentment, annoyance, and other petty sins that were not dealt with. And this turned into a deep resentment that eventually surfaced in a spectacular demolition of the home.

"Little sins" of irritation, displeasure, self-pity, and a critical spirit are like little swings with the sledge hammer. Eventually a wall gives way. Little sins always turn into big sins. Song of Songs says that the little foxes spoil the vineyard. Women need to have a zero-tolerance policy when it comes to their own sins. All must be repented of immediately. Lies must be confessed. Restitution must be made. Forgiveness must be sought in every case. Otherwise, one sin leads to another, and soon the things that should be the sweetest home comforts, the dinner table and the marriage bed, become stages for the impending tragedy to play out.

How can a woman seek out wisdom so this does not happen? How can she turn things around if the home is already in a state of rubble and confusion? As I said above, sin must first be recognized and dealt with. But next, she must consider the characteristics of wisdom as described in Proverbs and diligently seek it. "Do not be wise in your own eyes. Fear the Lord and depart from evil" (Prov. 3:7). The wise woman looks for wisdom from the Lord, not herself. This humility makes her teachable: "The

wise in heart will receive commands, but a prating fool will fall"
(10:8); "He who keeps instruction is in the way of life, but he
who refuses correction goes astray" (10:17). A foolish woman will
not receive commands, instruction, criticism, input, or correction
from anyone. Not from her husband, not from the pastor, not
from her friends, not from the Word. She is wise in her own eyes
and needs nothing. She justifies her behavior to herself. She tells
and retells her story in her own words and adjusts it to make sure
she is still the sympathetic character. But the other characters in
the story—her family—see her very differently.

The wise woman is not only teachable herself, but she teaches
others good things: "The tongue of the righteous is choice silver;
the heart of the wicked is worth little. The lips of the righteous
feed many, but fools die for lack of wisdom" (10:20–21). When
the wise woman speaks to her husband, it is nourishing. When
she talks with her children, they are blessed. She becomes a source
of strength to her family, rather than a drain on their joy. She is
a crown, bringing her husband "good and not evil all the days of
her life" (31:12).

A home with wisdom in it will be a "well of life" (10:11). A
woman who seeks this kind of wisdom will necessarily grow to
be cheerful, prudent, obedient, disciplined, respectful, and submissive to her husband, a blessing to all around her, building up
her home. This is in sharp contrast to the foolish woman who is
tearing down her house by being quarrelsome, noisy, indiscreet,
ignorant, self-indulgent, disputatious, argumentative, never satis-
fied, and always complaining. There is a reason for the repetition
in Proverbs on this subject: Women are prone to this common
temptation of being dripping faucets. And they radically underestimate the impact of their disobedience: "A continual dropping
on a very rainy day and a contentious woman are alike" (27:15).

Criticism That Kills

<><><><><><><><><><><><><><><><><><><><><><><><><><><><><><><><><><>

One of the great hindrances to Christian unity, whether in the home or in the community at large, is a critical, backbiting tongue. It is not just a "bad thing" that we generally ought to avoid; rather, as Paul says, it kills and destroys real people. Those people whom it crushes and drives away are most often our own parents, husbands, children, and our fellow saints who should be our friends.

I believe it was Spurgeon who said, "Fault finding is the easiest thing in the world." Backbiting is a work of the flesh; it is not a fruit of the Spirit. Wisdom and grace and maturity are not needed to have an eye to see the shortcomings of others. Any fool can see how others fall short. What requires wisdom is the ability to see our own sins and to think soberly of ourselves, not our normal fleshly tendency to think "more highly" of ourselves than we ought (Rom. 12:3).

Paul addresses this again in Philippians 2:3: "Let nothing be done through strife or vainglory; but in lowliness of mind let each esteem others better than themselves." Where there is criticism and backbiting, the root problem is always pride. The other associated sins may be jealousy and envy, but either way, pride is at the bottom. We have no need to learn to think much of ourselves, to care for ourselves, to consider our own needs, wants, and desires. We already do that far too much. The problem is getting us to think of others, to have a lowliness of mind that springs from humility and love.

Spurgeon also said, "Faults are thick where love is thin." God never said we would not live with people with faults. But He has told us that "love covers a multitude of sins" (1 Pet. 4:8). Peter says to "have fervent charity among yourselves." This is what is needed in a world full of sinners. Not just charity, but *fervent* charity. Criticizing and backbiting, rather than covering sin, expose it and breed more sin.

A critical spirit does not need to look far to find material for its favorite pastime of running people down. And because family members are usually in closest proximity, they get it the worst. Let's start with husbands. A wife commits the sin of backbiting when she runs her husband down to her parents, her children, her friends. She may laugh when she says these things, or she may tag "bless his heart" on the end of her remark, but when she shares his faults, his shortcomings, or his sins to others who have no need to know, she is sinning against the husband she is commanded to respect. This is one way a foolish woman tears down her house with her own hands (Prov. 14:1).

A wife can kill her husband with criticism to his face as well as behind his back. This comes in many forms: complaining, arguing, attributing motives, not responding, sighing, rolling her eyes, or ignoring. A critical spirit says, "You are not meeting my needs. You are not being a spiritual leader. You are not being a good husband or father. You are not providing for me the way I want. I wish you were more like so-and-so." This is the kind of wife Proverbs describes as being a drippy faucet (19:13). And it's no wonder a man would rather live in the desert or up on the roof than in the same house with such a cantankerous woman.

But this is the point where women begin to justify. "I know that's all true, but you don't know my husband. You don't know what a poor leader he is." Even if he is an unbeliever, Scripture tells women how to live with difficult husbands. It is always sinful to run people down in this manner, and it is especially sinful when it is the man who is to receive honor and respect from you. We do not render obedience to God only when we think it is a good idea; we are to obey God with a whole heart all the time in every circumstance by the grace He provides. Once we compromise, it is a slippery slope into many other sins. In this case, a wife is alienating the one who should be the closest to her. Then she wonders why he isn't very loving toward her.

Of course all of this applies to other family members as well. Mothers who glibly criticize their children are driving them away. When they do this to their face, it is destructive and alienating. When they criticize them to their friends, it is spreading the devastation even further. Children should receive our input in a loving manner, and only after much has been covered with love. But there is no excuse for parents to share negative things about their children to anyone else. This springs from a self-righteous "I have been wronged" attitude that is looking for pity. Sometimes it can come from a desire to lord it over our children or to try to maintain some kind of control, but it can never come from a charitable, merciful, gracious spirit.

Finally, repent of a critical, backbiting spirit. If you have sinned with your mouth, repent and make restitution. Do not say you were just joking. Confess to God that you have a proud spirit and seek to be lowly of mind. Seek forgiveness of your husband or your children, and by all means go to your friends who have heard you speak unkindly and seek their forgiveness as well. Ask God to cover your own sins and ask Him for love to cover the sins of those around you. This is the only way to rescue a marriage or family from impending destruction. It may not be too late to turn back the awful results of a backbiting spirit.

The Pricklies

No one I know really *enjoys* correction and reproof, and yet Scripture teaches that we are to receive it as a good thing. Proverbs 3:11–12 tells us not to "despise the chastening of the Lord, nor detest His correction" because it is a sign of His Fatherly love for us. Proverbs also tells us that "he who refuses correction goes astray" (10:17b) and "he who hates correction is stupid" (12:1b). Second Timothy 3:16 tells us Scripture "is profitable for reproof [and] for correction" and God uses this to complete us, equipping us "for every good work." In other words, without correction we are ill-equipped to do the good works God has prepared for us to walk in.

Most of us would agree: We are happy to take reproof from God; it's just when we receive it from fellow believers that we squawk. However, God seldom directly corrects us, unless we see it ourselves in the Scriptures, but He does use His people as a means to admonish and instruct each other. This is the biblical pattern, whether it comes from our pastors and teachers or from our fellow Christians. The correction can come by means of a sermon, an article, a tape, a book, or directly from a person in a private conversation. Women often react to correction in one of several, prickly, negative ways instead of receiving it as from the Lord for their good.

Let me give some examples. One negative way to react is by automatically getting defensive without even hearing the conclusion of the matter or finishing the article. Proverbs 18:13 says, "He who answers a matter before he hears it, it is folly and shame to him." If you react in such a way, you may be the one who really needs to hear it. If you hear a sermon about shoplifting and you have never shoplifted in your life, then chances are you won't be defensive about it at all. But if the topic is about anger, and you know you are sharp with your children on a regular basis, the temptation will be to start defending yourself instead of hearing the correction and finding help for your problem. Be sure to take note of your reactions, and remember that those corrections that annoy you the most may be the ones you most need to hear. Someone has said that if you throw a rock into a pack of dogs, the one that yelps is the one that got hit.

Another negative reaction is to be quick to criticize or blame the one bringing the correction. If you dismiss the speaker as pompous or inept (Who does he think he is? Does he think he's perfect or something?) simply because he has stepped on your toes, you may be rejecting some necessary correction that would be good for your soul. Again, check your reactions. Do you attribute bad motives to the one who brings a correction? This is a way of changing the subject so you don't have to deal with the correction.

Here's an example. Suppose someone comes to correct you about your tongue. Instead of listening and hearing the criticism out, you jump in and point out that it was really the people you told who were the talebearers. They should not have been carrying the gossip to the person now correcting you. Or you blame it on the people who told you in the first place. This is an old, old habit. Adam used it in the garden ("She gave it to me"); and Eve used it in the garden ("It was the serpent").

Often when we react to a correction, we say or do things we later regret. We dismiss the person by bringing up their own unrelated faults; we get on the phone before we have gotten a right attitude; we fire off a letter that we should have sat on for two or three days; we justify ourselves and assume a self-righteous attitude on the part of the person bringing the correction. Remember what Proverbs says: "He who hates correction is stupid."

One of the dangers of email is that it can be written hastily and fired off with no way of retrieval. Writing something on paper takes more deliberation and care. It has to be addressed and stamped and mailed, all great delayers in the process.

All these reactions to correction and reproof seem to point to the fact that the correction must be needed very much. If it wasn't needed, it would not have gotten such a spectacular reaction.

When correction and reproof come, Christian women ought to determine always to hear it out. Pray for grace to sit still through it. Then thank the person bringing it and tell them you will certainly think about what they have said. If they are dead wrong, there is no reason for you to be defensive. This goes back to the sermon on shoplifting. If you haven't done it, why get angry and defensive? If the correction is dead center, you only compound your fault by lashing out at the one bringing it.

If God's Word is true, correction and reproof are helpful in our growth and sanctification. A humble and meek Christian receives correction and carefully examines it before automatically rejecting it. Correction and reproof offend our pride. We do not mind seeing and correcting faults in others, but we do not want others to see or correct faults in us. This is being double-minded. Though we should be quick to overlook faults in others, we should not be so quick to overlook our own. And if we don't want others to have to correct us, we should be quick to correct ourselves.

Rainy-Day Blues

Okay, so it's a gray day. It's drizzling outside, or maybe it's even pouring rain. Maybe it's one of those days where it feels like it might rain any minute. And I'm not talking about one of those glorious summer thunderstorms that are so exciting to watch from the window, but rather just a muggy, bleak, very wet day. Whatever the case, it's easy to let the drizzle creep inside. The kids are a little whiny. Nobody will eat their breakfast. Squabbles are lurking, and the atmosphere is heavy with foreboding—this will be a day of dreariness. Mom may even be a little irritable. Let's face it—everyone has days like this. And when you are a mom at home with little ones, you need to be prepared to fend off the drizzle and keep it outside. After all, God made the rain and it's good, but it doesn't belong in the house. In other words, God doesn't want His children to be drooping and moping around, rain or not.

Some people love rainy, gray weather; it makes them feel cozy and snug when it is raining outside. But for most of us, bad weather brings our spirits down while sunshine lifts them up. We feel naturally more motivated, more cheerful, and more energetic when there is blue sky. But God has told us to take heed to our spirit. We have to be alert to those things that affect us, and we have to learn how to overcome the things that tend to make us feel crabby. And moms in particular need to learn how to shepherd all the little people in the house by keeping the rain outside.

The first thing of course is to know your own frame. If you are not affected in any way by the weather, then you have a head start. And if a rainy day doesn't bring any blues to your house, then you can skip the rest of this article. Or maybe other things bring the dampness in: Dad's gone on a business trip, the grandparents just left after a wonderful visit, everyone has the flu, or maybe it's just the letdown after Christmas or a birthday. Whatever the case, Mom needs to keep her own spirit in order before she can manage the kids.

Next, it is essential to know your own children. Moms really have a part in shaping their children's dispositions. The way you react to the weather teaches your children to do the same. We are creatures and not blocks of wood. The world around us affects us. We have to learn to apply wisdom in every situation and not "spiritualize" every temptation. Sometimes we need to overcome temptation by prayer and receiving grace; other times we need to put on some cheery music, open the curtains, and make a pot of coffee. God has given us the blessing of food when we are hungry, Advil when we have a headache, and Starbucks when we need a serious perk-up. We should avail ourselves of these blessings with gratitude to God our Creator, and not think we are somehow being unspiritual if we look to His creation for help and comfort.

Moms can minister to their children in similar ways. If everyone is droopy and cross, Mom may need to get creative to steer things in a more cheerful direction. First, you need to be cheerful yourself. Put some chocolate syrup in the kids' milk for breakfast—that's starting out on the right foot. Let them stay in their jammies a little longer than usual and make them a fort out of blankets in the living room. Pull out the dress-up box or the rainy-day coloring books. Bake some cookies. Be extravagant with the bubble bath and float a bowl of fruit loops in the tub with them. Make or buy some new Play-Doh and get out the cookie cutters. Use the red napkins at dinner. Put some flowers on the table. You get the idea—sometimes all that's needed is a little comfort and playfulness.

This might be fine and good with the little kids, but what about the school-age kids? True, they still need to go to school or hit the books at home. But you can send them out the door cheerfully with a good breakfast and a jolly hug. And if you are schooling the kids at home, you can still light the candles and make their studies bright and pleasant by having a happy countenance and demeanor yourself. Bring them a snack or a cup of cocoa for a break. Read some poetry together. Go for a walk in the rain. Let them stomp in the puddles. Get soaked.

We know that only the Spirit of God can bring real joy and happiness to our souls. But when we find that joy challenged by dreary circumstances, we have an obligation to overcome it with a wisdom grounded in faith. "Happy are the people whose God is the Lord!" (Ps. 144:15). As God's people, we want to lay aside the hindrances of sin and take James's (5:13) advice: "Is anyone cheerful? Let him sing psalms."

Put away any murmuring about the weather. It is unworthy of a Christian and a waste of time. Not only that, but it is a setup for other sins like laziness, self-pity, or envy. It only makes things worse, it distracts us away from our God-given duties, and it is mighty unproductive. Rather, we should ask God to stir up our hearts to joy and thanksgiving. This pleases Him and blesses us. Ask Him to help you manage your household joyfully. And when rain brings a case of the blues, break out the good spirits and glad comfort, and let the kids slosh around in it.

More from Canon Press

◇◇◇

Raining

You're sleeping before graveyard, and I'm alone with the rain, long and slow like time. I put my book down, to listen.

This is the last rain of the warm season, according to Ida Belle and Hattie who were out on their porch when I was shaking my dustmop this afternoon. They know all sorts of mysteries: the dangers of dog days, secrets of having a girl child, tricks for rooting flowers. Behind the rain I hear frozen trees scraping against the house and the stomp of your snow-packed boots on the mat.

By winter we will love each other more but I don't see how. In one brief summer I have forgotten what it was like to be single. Why do you sleep so long?

Maybe we can go camping in the mountains soon, before the first frost. In the dark tent we'll cling and make a knot against the vastness.

The deep says we are eternal. I cannot take it in. Only the rain unbroken teaches me just now that we will be lovers forever.

Sketches of Home
by Suzanne Clark

LaVergne, TN USA
11 December 2009
166701LV00003B/9/P